EARLY MARRIAGES, WILLS, AND SOME REVOLUTIONARY WAR RECORDS BOTETOURT COUNTY, VIRGINIA

Compiled by
ANNE LOWRY WORRELL

CLEARFIELD

Reprinted for
Clearfield Company, Inc. by
Genealogical Publishing Co., Inc.
Baltimore, Maryland
2004

Originally published: Hillsville, Virginia, 1958
Reprinted, with permission of the compiler, by
Genealogical Publishing Co., Inc.
1001 N. Calvert St., Baltimore, Md. 21202
1975, 1976, 1980, 1985, 1996
Reprinted from a volume in the
Virginia State Library, Richmond

Marriage Records of Botetourt County

Abbott, John, and Nancy Greenway, dau. George Greenway—Dec. 26, 1805.

Able, Henry, and Sarah Franklin, dau. Nathan Franklin—Aug. 31, 1816.

Able, Jeremiah, and Hannah Eakins—March 16, 1791. (Able was Rev. soldier.)

Able, John. (see Abbott above. Min. return gave ABLE, not Abbott.)

Able, John, and Elizabeth Hypes, Nicholas Hypes, surety—Jan. 17, 1793.

Abshire, Randolph, and Sara Cook, dau. Jacob Cook—Feb. 24, 1817.

Aby, Christian, and Nancy Richardson, widow Thomas Richardson, of Montgomery Co.—May 19, 1810.

Acton, Philip, and Elener Young, dau. William Young, dec.—Sept. 19, 1810.

Acton, William, and Margaret Compton—April 16, 1780.

Adams, Henry, and Sarah Clark, dau. Andrew Clark—April 2, 1793.

Adams, Joseph, and Elizabeth Seagraves. Samuel Seagraves, surety—Aug. 14, 1792.

Adams, William, and Agatha Strother Lewis, dau. William Lewis—Jan. 18, 1811.

Adkins, Edward, and Mary Wammucks—Oct. 1, 1810.

Adkins, John, and Mary Brannamer, dau. Anthony Brannamer—Jan. 30, 1804.

Adkins, William, and Mary Hartman—July 30, 1800.

Akins, Joseph, and Rosanna Caldwell. John Caldwell, surety—Feb. 14, 1787.

Albright, Cacper, and Charlotte Camper — April 19, 1791.

Albright, Henry, and Sarah Seawell, dau. Thomas Seawell—March 25, 1811.

Albright, John, and Polly Hash. Peter Hash, surety—Sept. 28, 1799.

Alderson, Burr, and Elizabeth Dawson—Feb. 18, 1797.

Alderson, Joseph, and Mary Newman, dau. Jonathan Newman—Jan. 5, 1789.

Alderson, Simon, and Ann Spratt—Aug. 16, 1773.

Alderson, Thomas, and Martha Moore, dau. James Moore. Thomas son of Curtis Alderson—July 13, 1789.

Alexander, James, and Mary Depew. Elijah Depew, surety—Dec. 24, 1793.

Alford, Henry, and Elinor Milling, dau. James Milling, Sr.—Aug. 9, 1802.

Alford, Thomas, and Betsy Miller. James Miller, surety—Sept. 29, 1797.

Alford, Thomas,, and Phebe Cummings, dau. Robert Cummings—Oct. 13, 1793.

All, Auld, Awl.

All, Alexander, and Nancy Shewsberry, dau. Dabney Shewsberry, dec.—June 8, 1811.

All, James, and Esther Duncan, dau. Robert Duncan, dec.—Jan. 11, 1803.

All, James, and Nancy Beckner, dau. A. Beckner, dec.—Nov. 5, 1805.

All, John, and Hannah McClenchan—April 12, 1803.

Allen, Archabald, and Anna Colbreath, dau. John Colbreath—March 4, 1815.

Allen,, Malcolm, and Margaret Henderson, dau. Mary Henderson—Jan. 4, 1794.

Allen, John, and Hannah King—March 20, 1800.

Allen, John, and Patsy Allen, dau. John Allen—Aug. 28, 1807.

Allen, Robert, and Jane Hill—March 10, 1784.

Allen, Robert, and Frances Harvey, dau. Robert Harvey—Oct. 15, 1822.

Allen, Solomon, and Susanna Stevens, dau. John Stevens (Montgomery Co.)—May 15, 1787.

Allen, William, and Caroline Poage, dau. George Poage—May 17, 1819.

Allen, William, and Mary Kelley—June 18, 1806. (Dau. George, dec., and Mary Kelley or Keller.)

Alverson, John, and Mary Ovenchain, widow of George Ovenchain—Jan. 27, 1818.

Amon, Ammen, Amen.

Amon, Daniel, and Catherine Hesston, June 11, 1796.

Amon, David, and Sarah Houtts, dau. Christopher Houtts—Sept. 6, 1802.

Amon, John, and Christina Beckner, widow Abraham Beckner—Sept. 10, 1810.

Amon, Michael, and Catherine Deardorf, dau. Peter Deardorf—April 5, 1791.

Amos, Isaac, and Polly Boyer, dau. Devault

Boyer, dec.—Aug. 17, 1803.

Anderson, Geroge C. and Polly Douglas, dau. Benjamin Douglas, Sr.—Sept. 25, 1804.

Anderson, James, and Maryann Tathum, dau. John Tathum—May 1789.

Anderson, James, and Ann Sharkey. James Sharkey, surety—March 3, 1797.

Anderson, James, and Nancy Reynolds, dau. William Reynolds, dec.—Feb. 2, 1807.

Anderson, John, and Martha Broadwater— July 22, 1800.

Anderson, John, and Rebecca Maxwell—Jan. 10, 1775.

Anderson, John, and Ann McClure. Yjos Anderson, surety — Nov. 29, 1791.

Anderson, John, and Ann Awl—March 16, 1791.

Anderson, John, and Matilda Wax, dau. Henry Wax—Jan. 20, 1820.

Anderson, Joseph, and Sarah Biss (Bip)— Feb. 6, 1780.

Anderson, Joseph, and Catherine Wilson— Oct. 12, 1793.

Anderson, Joseph, and Christinah Britz, dau. Adam Britz—Aug. 31, 1845.

Anderson, Joseph, and Mary Newman. Jonathan Newman and John Anderson, sureties—Jan. 5, 1789.

Anderson, Robert, and Elizabeth Lemmon. Christopher Lemmon, surety—April 2, 1801.

Anderson, Samuel, and .... McKee— April 21, 1794.

Anderson, Simon, and Ann Spratt—Aug. 11, 1773.

Anderson, Thomas, and Rebecca McClure. Malcolm McClure, surety—Feb. 12, 1784.

Anderson, William, and Deborah Harris, dau. Thomas Harris—June 21, 1810.

Andrews, James, and Nancy Bishop, dau. Jeremiah Bishop—Aug. 14, 1811.

Andrews, Samuel, and Mary McKee—1794. (See Anderson above.)

Angel, William, and Hurldy Stanley, dau. Pleasant Stanley—Aug. 1, 1811.

Arbuckle, Matthew, and Frances Lawrence, widow—Dec. 17, 1774.

Arbuckle, William, and Katerine Poague. George Poague, surety—Nov. 11, 1779.

Archy, Joseph, and Elizabeth Lefford, dau. Peter Lefford—March 24, 1807.

Armentrout, Frederick, and Betsy Wolf. John Wolf, surety—April 22, 1799.

Armstrong, Alexander, and Elizabeth Hume —May 10, 1820.

Armstrong, Alexander, and Pricilla Robinson, dau. Joseph Robinson—Sept. 12, 1792.

Armstrong, George, and Elizabeth Green.

James Green, surety—Sept. 8, 1801.

Armstrong, James, and Mary Thompson. Concent by Martha Thompson—June 20, 1787.

Armstrong, Phares, and Jane Harris, dau. John Harris—Sept. 27, 1819.

Armstrong, Thomas, and Elizabeth Critz. Jacob Critz, surety—Nov. 28, 1801.

Armstrong, William D., and Elizabeth Buckhannon, widow Thedor Buckhannon—Jan. 17, 1820.

Armstrong, William, and Catherine Moore, dau. William Moore—Nov. 31, 1818.

Arnett, Michael, and Mary Woolf, dau. John Woolf—Jan. 4, 1795 (min. return - 1791).

Arnett, Thomas (son Thomas) and Martha McFerran, dau. Aynush McFerran—May 11, 1791.

Asberry, William (son of James of Bedford Co.), and Oney Simmons, dau. Polly Simmons—Jan. 30, 1819.

Ashford, William, and Mary Thompson—Feb. 27, 1785.

Aston, see Acton.

Atchey, Martanno, and Zephery Taylor—Feb. 1785.

Athan, Lasley Fairfax, and Mary Beechwax. Samuel Beechwax, surety—Sept. 10, 1795.

Aunspaugh, Charles, and Harriet Fleager, dau. Michael Fleager—Nov. 11, 1822.

Aversole, Jacob, and Sarah Keller, dau John Keller—May 11, 1803.

—B—

Baber, G. Washington, and Sally Steele, dau. George Steele—March 30, 1822.

Backensto, John, and Elizabeth James, dau. Allen James—Jan. 1, 1818.

Backey, Andrew, Jr., (under age), and Susanna Kinzey, dau. Christian Kinzey—July 11, 1805.

Bacley, Andrew, and Sally Paxton, dau. Thomas Paxton, dec.—July 20, 1805.

Baker, Caleb, and Lucy Cooper, dau. Sarah Cooper—Oct. 1, 1821.

Baker, John, and Anna Sophia Snider, widow —Nov. 24, 1804.

Baker, Martin, and Phebe Snodgrass—Feb. 11, 1772.

Baldwin, Samuel, and Mary Wills. William Bandy, Richard, and Lucy Justice—May 23, 1794.

Bandy Richard, and Nancy Lewellen, dau Thomas Lewellen—Sept. 3, 1791.

Bandy, Richard, and Elizabeth Henry, dau. William Henry—Dec. 7, 1816.

Bandy, Solomon, and Mary Barnett—April 9, 1799

Bandy, Thomas, and Nancy Craddock, dau. William Craddock, dec.—April 16, 1806.

Barber, John, and Ann Cunningham, dau. Thomas Cunningham—May 24, 1821.

Barnard, Shubal J., and Peggy McClure, niece William Blain—Dec. 19, 1816.

Barnhart, William, and Polly White—May 20, 1798.

Barnes, Benjamin, and Sarah Smith—June 3, 1801.

Barnes, Thomas, and Ingy Ruddle—Nov. 24, 1799.

Barnett, David, and Mary Wallace. Consent by James Reyburn, guardian—April 14, 1789.

Barnett, John, ("21 the 26 inst."), and Sarah Billups, dau. Edward Billups—March 25, 1809.

Barnett, John, and Ann Deyerle—Sept. 10, 1783.

Barnett, John, and Marjore Henry. William Henry, surety—May 24, 1793.

Barnett, William, and Ann Miller. Thomas Miller, surety—Nov. 25, 1793. Wills, surety—March 10, 1778.

Barnhart, William, and Polly White—May 20, 1798.

Barrett, Luke, and Mary Smith, dau. Jacob Smith—Oct. 30, 1816.

Barrett, William, and Elizabeth Evans. (Marriage return says Eliz. Coons)—Nov. 26, 1783.

Bartlett, John, and Estha Hinkle, "ward and daughter-in-law of Jacob Garst"—April 18, 1813.

Bartley, Hugh, and Sarah Culbertson—Sept. 1, 1772.

Barton, Samuel, and Martha Robertson. Consent by Jas. Woods—March 10, 1778.

Barton, William, and Sarah Howard, dau. John and Ann Howard—Aug. 19, 1794.

Baughman, John, and Dolly Moyer, dau. Jacob Moyer—July 21, 1805.

Baxter, George, and Ann Fleming, dau. William and Ann Fleming—July 17, 1778.

Bayne, James, and Mary French, dau. William French—April 30, 1814.

Beagler, John, and Maryann Henry, dau. William Henry—May 24, 1800.

Beale, Charles, and Elizabeth Skillern, dau. Capt. George Skillern—Aug. 8, 1797.

Beale, Charles, and Anna Kyle, dau. William Kyle—Sept. 1, 1807.

Beale, George S., and Elizabeth Lewis, dau. Capt William Lewis—Nov. 15, 1814.

Beale, John, and Peggy Skillern, dau. Capt. George Skillern—Uov. 17, 1788.

Beale, Madison T. and Charlotte Poage, dau. George Poage—Nov. 17, 1810.

Bear, Gadip, and Eve Feller, dau. Peter Feller—Feb. 24, 1810.

Beard, Thomas, and Martha Wilson, dau. Thomas and Jean Wilson—Aug. 12, 1794.

Beard, William, and Sussana Potts—Aug. 21, 1793.

Beath, Joseph, and Barbara Moomaw, dau. John Moomaw—April 27, 1794.

Beaubeau, John, and Abagail Waggoner, dau. Christopher Waggoner—Feb. 1, 1802.

Beckett, John (son of Richard and Susanna), and Anne Becklesimer, dau. John and Eliz. —Dec. 17, 1788.

Beckner, Daniel and Elizabeth Evans, dau. William Evans—Nov. 18, 1822.

Beckner, Daniel, and Elizabeth Gross—1796.

Beckner, David, and Hannah Gross. Adam Gross, surety—July 1, 1796.

Beckner, Henry, and Betsy Thomas,—Feb. 20, 1797.

Beckner, Henry, and Christinah Deardoff, dau. Peter Deardoff—Sept. 6, 1790.

Beckner, Henry, and Cathy O'tult, dau. George O'tult—July 7, 1807.

Beckner, Henry, and Christinah Beckner, dau. Nicholas Beckner—1790.

Beckner, Isaac, and Catherine Corfman, dau. Peter Corfman, dec.—Dec. 23, 1805.

Beckner, Jacob, and Mary Thrasher, dau. Frederick Thrasher—Feb. 21, 1820.

Beckner, John, and Elizabeth Cook, dau. John Cook—Oct. 12, 1820.

Beckner, John, and Elizabeth Gish, dau. George Gish—Sept. 9, 1804.

Beckner, John, and Mary Harshbarger, dau. Christopher Harshbarger—Oct. 12, 1809.

Beckner, John, and Mary Duncan, dau. Robert Duncan, dec.—Aug. 15, 1800.

Beckner, Joseph, and Jean Moore—March 28, 1799.

Beckner, Joseph, and Susanna Seacrist, dau. John Seacrist—Dec. 30, 1817.

Beckner, Joseph, and Elizabeth Feller, dau. Peter Feller, dec.—Oct. 28, 1811.

Beckner, Samuel, and Sarah Spitler, dau. Michael Spitler—April 8, 1822.

Beesaker, Adam, and Boarbara Coap, dau. Jacob Coap (consent in German)—Nov. 18, 1794.

Bell, Jeremiah, and Elizabeth Saver—June 14, 1796.

Bell, John, and Catherine Newman, dau. Benjamin Newman—April 6, 1818.

Bennett, Isaac, and Jane Defore, dau. John Defore—May 2, 1804.

Bennett, Jacob, and Mary Persinger. Henry Persinger, surety—May 31, 1800.

Bennett, John, and Sarah Clancy—Nov. 26, 1782.

Bennett, Moses, and Nancy Cooper, dau. William Cooper—Jan. 20, 1805.

Bennett, William, and Margaret Price, dau. Thomas Price—July 25, 1811.

Benny, John, and Mary Price—Dec. 27, 1781.

Bess, William, and Rebeckah Hammilton—April 23, 1799.

Beuford, John, and Elinor McGowin, dau. Paul McGowin—April 22, 1802.

Bickers, James, and Mary Johnson. John Johnson, surety—Jan. 20, 1782.

Bickle, James, and Rebecca Bridgeland—Feb. 20, 1816.

Biggs, Caleb, and Mary Hanson—Jan 2, 1799.

Biggs, David, and Jemima Guliver—Jan. 22, 1799.

Biggs, Thomas, and Rachel Gulliford (over 21). Randall Biggs, surety—Sept. 16, 1802.

Biggs, William, and Elizabeth Caldwell, dau. Caldwell—May 29, 1807.

Bilbro, John, and Jane Crawford, dau. Josiah Crawford—Jan. 18, 1807.

Bilbro, Thomas, and Elizabeth Nofsinger, dau. Samuel Nofsinger—March 30, 1812.

Billups, Edward, and Mary Howell—Aug. 27, 1796.

Billups, William (son Edward), and Jane Garwood, (21)—Dec. 31, 1813.

Bird, William, and Rebekah Allen, dau. Moses Allen—April 18, 1805.

Bird, William Norman, and Mary Fisher, dau. John Fisher—Jan. 11, 1802.

Bird, William, and Polly Jerrett—Jan. 12, 1802.

Bish, George W., and Susannah Nofsinger, dau Joseph Nofsinger, dec.—Sept 10, 1816.

Bishop, John, and Elizabeth Fought, dau. John Faught—June 26, 1806.

Black, Frederick, Jr., and Susannah Snyder. Father dead—Nov. 20, 1804.

Black, Jacob, and Barbara Lark (over 21)—Jan. 26, 1796.

Black, Samuel, and Lucy Boone, April 1, 1801.

Black, Samuel, and Agnes Rowland, dau. James Rowland, dec—April 8, 1807.

Black, William, and Anne McDonald, dau. Edward McDonald—Nov. 20, 1817.

Blackwell, Henry, and Hannah Burns—Oct. 22, 1818.

Blain, Alexander (of Albemarle Co.. Va.),

and Lucinda Walton, dau. William Walton—Jan. 9, 1809.

Blain, William, and Elizabeth Hook, dau. Henry Hook, dec.—Sept. 26, 1817.

Blain, William, and Esther Carlton, dau. James Carlton—March 31, 1817.

Blaze, William, and Catherine Englehard, dau. George Englehard—Aug. 19, 1806.

Bless, Christopher, and Anna Good, dau. Christopher Good—Nov. 12, 1819.

Board, Nathan, and Sarah Cooper, dau. Charles Cooper—June 3, 1819.

Bockman, Henry, and Elizabeth Manners, dau. Christopher Manners—July 1, 1800.

Bofford, Samuel, and Sarah Shaver—Nov. 2, 1793.

Bogan, John, and Marian Wallace (over 21) —Nov. 12, 1798.

Bogess, David, and Sarah Woolf—April 21, 1800.

Bogess, George, and Jane Haynes—Aug. 22, 1793.

Bogess, Henry, and Polly Pitzer, dau. John Pitzer—Oct. 26, 1795.

Boswell, George, and Elizabeth Crowell, dau. Henry Crowell—Sept. 5, 1818.

Boindrager, David, and Elizabeth Spiller. Jacob Spiller, surety—Feb. 24, 1800.

Boindrager, James, and Susan Murray, dau. Frederick Murray—Jan. 23, 1816.

Bolton, Henry, and Nancy Mann—April 5, 1799.

Bolton, Jacob, and Elizabeth Juksil, dau. John Juksil, dec.—March 20, 1816.

Bolton, Robert, and Hannah Long, dau. Thomas Long—April 9, 1819.

Bomgardner, Jacob, and Mary Sherrod, dau. Thomas Sherrod, March 15, 1817.

Bond, John, and Elizabeth Bryant (over 21). John Bryant, surety—April 2, 1796.

Bondsack, Jacob, and Catherine Harshbarger, dau. Samuel Harshbarger—Nov. 22, 1819.

Bondsack, John, and Susanna Harshbarger, dau. Samuel Harshbarger—May 27, 1816.

Bonner, Benjamin, and Sarah Smith—June 3, 1803.

Book, John, and Susannah Hook, dau. Peter Hook—Nov. 23, 1814.

Booker, Andrew, and Frances Bradley—Oct. 28, 1780.

Boose, Abraham, and Peggy Linkenhoger, dau. Elias Linkenhoger—May 11, 1814.

Booze, David, and Polly Huntsman, dau. Peter Huntsman, of Bedford Co., Va.,—July 21. 1816.

Bosford, Samuel, and Sarah Shavous, dau. Frederick Shavous (Shaver?)—Nov. 1, 1779.

Bosters, Jonathan, and Mary Huffman, dau. John Huffman—Feb. 24, 1815.

Henry Crowell—Sept. 5, 1818.

Boughman, Christopher, and Rachel Glasburn, dau. David Glasburn—May 3, 1813.

Boughman, John, and Dolly Moyers, dau. Jacob Moyers—Feb. 9, 1805.

Boughman, John, and Betsy Cox, dau. John Cox—Nov. 22, 1820.

Boulteon, Peter, and Polly Foltz, dau. James Foltz—Dec. 26, 1821.

Bow, James, and Sarah McCahan, widow of Andrew McCowan—Sept. 9, 1814.

Bowen, Labin, and Betsy Cooper, dau. Charles Cooper—Feb. 25, 1811.

Bowen, Labin, and Betsy Henderson, dau. John Henderson—Feb. 25, 1811.

Bowen, William, and Elizabeth Smith—Aug. 24, 1795.

Bower, Charles, and Elizabeth Shaver. Charles Shaver, surety—1794.

Bower, George, and Polly Shellenbarger—Aug. 15, 1822.

Bower, Jacob, and Barbara Hawbert, dau. George Hawbert—April 8, 1823.

Bowers, John, and Polly Gross. Adam Gross, surety—May 28, 1798.

Bower, Michael, and Betsy Hiner, dau. Anthony Hiner—March 15, 1822.

Bower, Nathias, and Catherine Linkenhoger —Aug. 8, 1817.

Bowers, Stopel, and Catherine Walter, dau. Martin Walter, Oct. 1, 1817.

Bower, William, and Agnes Brickey, dau. Peter Brickey—May 11, 1813.

Bower, William, and Katherine Kessler, dau. Jacob Kessler—May 10, 1813.

See Bowyer.

Bowman, Peter, and Elizabeth Bishop, dau. Jeremiah Bishop—Sept. 27, 1803.

Bowyer, Adam, and Christinah Woolf. John Woolf, surety—Nov. 7, 1794.

Bowyer, Christopher, and Sarah Weaver, dau. Leonard Weaver—Aug. 13, 1816.

Bowyer, David and Sarah Woolf—April 21, 1820.

Bowyer, Henry, and Matilda Breckenridge. daughter James Breckenridge—Sept. 12, 1820.

Bowyer, Henry, and Agatha Madison, dau. Thomas Madison—Aug 9, 1792.

Bowyer, John, and Polly Cahoon. Charles Cahoon, surety—March 9, 1802.

Bowyer, John M., and Polly M. Lewis, dau. William Lewis—Sept. 3, 1816.

Bowyer, William C., and Lucy A. Burwell, dau. Nathaniel Burwell, dec.—Dec. 28, 1811.

See Bower.

Boyd, Alexander C., and Catherine Tutwilder, dau. Jacob and Catherine Tutwilder—Oct. 11, 1813.

Boyd, James, anl Mary Bryan, dau. William Bryan—June 28, 1813.

Boyd, John, and Susanna Hiner. Jacob Hiner, surety—June 28, 1803.

Boyle, Abraham, and Margaret McClanahan, dau. William and Margaret McClanahan—Dec. 5, 1796.

Bozman, John, and Catherine Pifley, dau David Pifley—Feb. 21, 1815.

Brace, Peter, and Charity Emmons, dau. William Emmons—Jan. 14, 1790.

Bradford (see Bradley)

Bradford, Edward, and Mary Keller, dau. Adam Keller, dec.—Dec. 28, 1813.

Bradford, John, and Sarah Grimley. John Bradford, Sr., surety—Aug. 4, 1800.

Bradford, Joseph, and Jane Drummond, dau. George Drummond—Jan. 24, 1818.

Bradley, John, and Acey Johnson, widow— May 4, 1790.

Bradley, John, and Maria Fogg—Sept. 25, 1817.

Bradley, Joshua, and Spicey Cruz, dau. James Cruz—Oct. 31, 1807.

Bradshaw, Isaac, and Polly Crush, "alias Polly Thompson"—Aug. 8, 1815.

Bragg, John, and Patsy C. Robinson, dau. Lewis Robinson—May 19, 1820.

Branamer, Conrad, and Caty Bishop, dau. Jeremiah Bishop—April 13, 1813.

Bratcher, Jenjamin, and Elizabeth Ferrill (21). Babriel Ferrill, surety—Sept. 13, 1803.

Bratton, James, and Dorethea Fleming, dau. Col. Wm. and Ann Fleming—April 23, 1800.

Bratton, Thomas, and Polly Jordon, dau. Thomas Jordon—Dec. 28, 1809.

Breadwell, William, and Sarah Brown, dau. William Brown—Nov. 15, 1806.

Breedlove, Isaac, and Sarah Miller, dau. John Brown—Jan. 4, 1819.

Brian-Briant, etc.

Brians, Charles, and Ann Fausher Hudnall, dau. Ezekiah Hudnall—Aug. 16, 1805.

Brians, James, and Elizabeth Vineyard, dau. Christian Vineyard—Dec. 28, 1793.

Brians, James, and Rachel Andtrson, dau. Burr Anderson—June 5, 1815.

Brians, John, and Jane Livingston, dau. Wm. Livingston—Jan. 2, 1796.

Bryan, Stephen, and Susanna Melone, dau. Thomas—Jan. 9, 1813.

Brians, William, and Pricilla Graham, dau. Frances Graham, dec.—Dec. 31, 1793.

Brickey, James, and Mary Johnson—Jan. 20, 1782.

Brickey, Jarrett, and Mary Slinker. dau. John Slinker—1789.

Brickey, John, and Rhoda Shewsberry, dau. Dabney Shewsberry—March 7, 1818.

Brickey, John, and Elizabeth Richason, dau. William Richeson—Jan. 6, 1818.

Brickey, Peter, and Rebeckah Hartman, dau. Nicholas Hartman, dec.—March 20, 1814.

Brickey, Samuel, and Sally Buckhannon, dau. Theadore Buckhannon—March 24, 1814.

Briggs, John, and Tomsey Jones—April 23, 1783.

Bright, George, and Mary McNeil, dau. Daniel McNeil—April 24, 1805.

Bright, James, and Margaret Smith. John Smith, surety—May 5, 1778.

Brimmer, Anthony, and Magdalene Pitzer, dau. Abraham Brimmer—Nov. 6, 1820.

Brinkey, John, and Ruth Saintclear—Oct. 8, 1780.

Britz, Henry, and Catherine Frantz, dau. Michael Frantz—June 3, 1802.

Britz, Samuel, and Catherine Ground, dau. George Ground—Dec. 11, 1821.

Broils, Solomon, and Isabella Eakin, dau. Nathan Eakin—Sept. 19, 1816.

Bronaman, Conrad, and Barbara Treslar. Henry Treslar, surety, Jan. 25, 1795.

Bronaman, Conrad, and Caty Bishop, dau. Jeremiah Bishop—April 13, 1813.

Bronaman, George, and Mary Drake, dau. John Drake—Aug. 23, 1810.

Bronaman, Peter, and Elizabeth Bishop, dau. Jeremiah Bishop—Sept. 27, 1803.

Brooks, Jonathan, and Margaret Reyburn—Oct. 20, 1789.

Brooks, Lawson, and Catherine Moyers, dau. George Moyers—Aug. 26, 1820.

Brooks, Tunis, and Sarah Hartman, dau. John Hartman—Jan. 24, 1815.

Brooks, Tunis, and Peggy French, dau. William French—April 30, 1816.

Brough, Abraham, and Barbara Coffmon, dau. Henry Coffmon—May 6, 1817.

Brough, Daniel, and Catherine Painter, dau. Henry Painter—Aug. 28, 1818.

Brough, Harmon, and Mary Painter, dau. Henry Painter—July 29, 1797.

Brough, John, and Susanna Clark—May 17, 1815.

Brough, John, and Catherine Peters, dau. Jacob Peters—April 5, 1813.

Brough, John, and Catherine Blain, dau. George Blain—Sept. 24, 1816.

Brough, Peter, and Betsy Coffman, dau.

Henry Coffman—Nov. 11, 1806.

Brown, Cornelius, and Jane Rowland. James Rowland, surety—April 26, 1794.

Brown, Hezekiah, and Jane Bandy, dau. John Bandy—May 14, 1807.

Brown John, and Betsy Watkins, widow of James Watkins—Oct. 23, 1809.

Brown, John, and Adalaide Kyle, dau. Barclay Kyle—Sept. 14, 1818.

Brown, John, and Susanna Cowan. John Cowan, surety—March 16, 1799.

Brown, Lewis, and Betsy Patsall, dau. Jacob Patsall—Oct. 26, 1811.

Brown, Thomas, and Margaret Anderson--Jan. 22, 1779.

Brown, Thomas, and Susanna Terry, dau. William Terry—Jan. 21, 1783.

Brown, Thomas, and Nancy Litton—Nov. 5, 1795.

Brown, Thomas, and Ann Cartmill, dau. Henry Cartmill, Sr.—Aug. 29, 1815.

Brown, Walker, and Sarah Turner, dau. Dec. 3, 1803.

Brown, William, and Sarah Guy—Jan. 12, 1782.

Brown, William, and Patsy Dugins ("Over 21")—May 25, 1796.

Brown, William, and Susanna Spesard, dau. Michael Spesard—June 18, 1820.

Brownlee, James, and Polly Watkins, dau. Philip Watkins—Aug. 5, 1801.

Brubaker, Abraham, and Elizabeth Linkhough—Jan. 11, 1791.

Brubaker, Abraham, and Ann Dill, dau, Henry Dill—Sept. 2, 1816.

Brubaker, Adam, and Barbara Coap, dau. Jacob Coap—Nov. 19, 1794. Consent in German.

Brugh, See Brough.

Brunk, Jacob, and Nancy Shank, dau. Christian Shank—Oct. 10, 1806.

Brunnemer, Jacob, and Elizabeth Mallow, dau. Michael Mallow—Sept. 6, 1816.

Brush, John, and Catherine Trout, dau. Jacob Trout—Aug. 23, 1790.

Bryant (See Brian-Brians)

Bryant, Eppa, and Delila Franklin, dau. Edward Franklin—Oct. 10, 1820.

Bryant, James, and Margaret Welch—Dec. 9, 1779.

Bryant, James, and Elizabeth Lilies—Dec. 28, 1780.

Bryant, John, and Sarah Walker, dau. William Walker, dec.—Nov. 8, 1803.

Bryant, Lewis, and Nancy Short, dau. John Short, dec.—Aug. 17, 1818.

Bryant, Rowland, and Elizabeth Jones—Oct.

1, 1780.

Bryant, Rowland, and Nancy Ashley—Aug. 7, 1792.

Bryant, William, and Polly Arnett, dau. Thomas Arnett—Nov. 13, 1786.

Bryant, William, and Sarah Henry—Feb. 29, 1778.

Bryant, William, and Martha Lewis—March 11, 1784.

Bryant, William, and Elizabeth Phillips—June 6, 1785.

Bryant, William, and Catherine Pogue—1779.

Buchanan, John, and Sarah Mosly Leforce—Sept. 20, 1794.

Buchanan, Theadere, and Elizabteh Huntsman. Peter Huntsman surety—Oct. 4, 1800.

Buckingham, Richard, and Rachel Switzer, dau. Nathan Switzen—July 24, 1816.

Bunter, John, and Elizabeth Highlands—Sept. 8, 1797.

Burch, George, and Marv Hiley. William Hiley, surety—Dec. 31, 1788.

Burens, Henry, and Mary Miller. Peter Miller, surety—Feb. 11, 1788.

Burger, Henry, and Ann Warner, dau. Daniey Warner—March 27, 1795.

Burgess, Joseph, and Rebecca Seckingast, dau, Daniel Seckingast—Jan. 16. 1822.

Burk, Isham, and Elizabeth Rowland. Thomas Rowland, surety—Jan. 6, 1781.

Burk, Samuel, and Sarah Rowland. widow—March 1, 1778.

Burnett, Robert, and Elizabeth Gish, dau. John Gish—Jan. 18, 1811.

Burns, James, and Susanna Hughes, dau. Thomas Hughes— June 17, 1793.

Bussy, John, and Cecily Camper, dau. Solomon Camper—Dec. 13, 1809.

Butcher, John, and Selly Maddox, dau. Scholfield Maddox—March 5, 1802.

Butcher. Samuel (son of William), and Mary Burns, dau. Isaac Burns—Oct. 25, 1790.

Butcher, Samuel, and Mary Turner, dau. William Turner—Feb. 23, 1809.

Butler, Edward, and Elizabeth Deaton—Sept. 24, 1811.

Butler, George, and Margaret Coon, dau. Jacob Coon—Aug. 16, 1803.

Butler, William, and Rachel Darr, dau. Joseph Darr, Sr.—Sept. 8, 1804.

Butt. Abraham, and Margaret Caul, dau. James Caul—May 16, 1812.

Butt, Addison, and Eleanor Glenn, dau. James Glenn—May 19, 1802.

Buttrig, Robert, and Mary Daughtery—Nov. 23, 1797.

—C—

Cain, John, and Elizabeth Earhart, dau. Jacob Earhart—Feb. 20, 1819.

Caldwell, Allen, and Polly Allen, dau. John Allen—Sept. 19, 1804.

Caldwell, Alexander, and Margaret Looney, dau. Absolum Looney—July 25, 1778.

Caldwell, Andrew, and Susannah Hughes, dau. George Hughes—Jan. 19, 1813.

Caldwell, Archabald, and Elizabeth Mattenbarger, dau. William Mattenbarger—June 28, 1799.

Caldwell, Davis, and Nancy Farrier, dau. William Farrier, dec.—Nov. 10, 1818.

Caldwell, Edmundson, and Sarah Crist, dau. Philip Crist, March 31, 1811.

Caldwell, Granville, and Catherine Robinson —Aug. 9, 1814.

Caldwell, Henry, and Polly Farrier, dau. Robert Farrier—Dec. 17, 1803.

Caldwell, Hugh, and Betsy Deardorf, dau. Henry Deardorf—Oct. 3, 1803.

Caldwell, Hugh, and Nancy Farrier, dau. Robert Farrier—Oct. 9, 1809.

Caldwell, Jack, and Polly Brooks, widow of William Brooks—Nov. 10, 1817.

Caldwell, James, and Jane Weirs, widow of Thomas Weirs—June 6, 1818.

Caldwell, James, and Sarah Holt—May 29, 1791.

Caldwell, John, and Elizabeth Hanson. David Hanson, surety—Dec. 6, 1794.

Caldwell, John, and Mary Hively, dau. Jacob Hively—Oct. 22, 1804.

Caldwell, John, and Leah Newman. Aaron Newman, surety—Oct. 18, 1795.

Caldwell, Joseph, and Barbara Miltebarger, dau. William Miltebarger—April 11, 1808.

Caldwell, Robert, and Patsey Newman—Sept. 9, 1799.

Caldwell, Robert, and Mary Smith, dau. Jacob Smith—Sept. 4, 1813.

Caldwell, Samuel, and Sarah Holstein, dau. Henry Holstein, Sr.—April 14, 1812.

Caldwell, Stephen, and Elizabeth Weir—May 9, 1797.

Caldwell, William, and Elizabeth Hackett. Thomas Hackett, surety—Aug. 2, 1792.

Caldwell, William, and Pricilla Luney, dau. Absolum Luney—March 24, 1789.

Caldwell, William, and Polly (Fanny) Anderson, dau. Joseph Anlerson—March 30, 1813.

Cale (Cole), Thomas, and Martha Deaton, dau. Levi Deaton, of Amelia Co., Va.—

April 7, 1818.

Calhoun, James, and Nelly West, dau. Benjamin West—May 26, 1790.

Calhoun, John, and Elizabeth Jichower, dau. Samuel Jichower—April 22, 1811.

Calhoun, Robert H., and Elizabeth McCrery—May 29, 1815.

Callahan, Charles, and Nancy Persinger, dau. Jacob Persinger—Dec. 9, 1811.

Calvert, Samuel, and Eliza Douthat, dau. Robert Douthat—Feb. 15, 1820.

Cammell, James, and Polly Livingston, dau. William Livingston—May 25, 1803.

Campbell, Daniel, and Mary White, widow of Peter White—Jan. 25, 1812.

Campbell, George, and Nancy Carden. Joseph Carden, surety— March 9, 1790.

Campbell, Isaac, and Sarah Lapsley, dau. Joseph Lapsley—Aug. 18, 1773.

Campbell, James, and Sarah Vansant, dau. Sarah Vansant—1786.

Campbell. John, and Mary Gish, dau. Abraham Gish—June 30, 1819.

Campbell, John, and Elizabeth McDonald. Edward McDonald, surety—Jan. 10, 1778.

Campbell, Robert, and Rebecca McDonald, Edward McDonald, surety—Nov. 28, 1785.

Campbell, William, and Susannah Dabney—Feb. 14, 1781.

Campbell, William, and Patsy Bandy, dau. John Bandy—April 30, 1806.

Camper, David, and Cibline Camper, dau. Solomon, April 27, 1816.

Camper, Francis, and Susanna Jeyhawer, dau. Samuel Jeyhawer—May 20, 1811.

Camper, Harmon, and Hannah Camper—Nov. 25, 1801.

Camper, John, and Sally Lovel, dau. Edward Lovel—Jan. 25, 1806.

Camper, John, and Nancy Ovenchain, dau. Philip Ovenchain—March 1, 1807.

Camper, John, and Hannah Carney, widow of Patrick—May 26, 1817.

Camper, Peter, and Elinor Ovenchain, dau. Philip Ovenchain—March 1, 1817.

Camper, Sanford, and Catherine Sheets, dau. Jacob and Caty Sheets—Jan. 2, 1804.

Camper, Simon, and Polly Campbell—Jan. 11, 1809.

Camron, and Lydia Taylor, dau. Jonathan Taylor—1787.

Camron, John anl Lydia Snodgrass—Sept. 9, 1771.

Carden, Joseph, and Judith Kenner, dau. Robert (dec.) and Judith Kenner—Sept. 13, 1811.

Carlton, James, and Esther Brown, dau.

Thomas Brown—Aug. 26, 1806.

Carlton, William, and Margaret Prince, dau. Godfrey Prince—Oct. 14, 1805.

Carnes, George, and Elizabeth Persinger, dau. Christopher Persinger—April 26, 1794.

Carnes, John, and Elizabeth Gillihand, dau. James and Susannah Gillihand. dec.—April 16, 1813.

Carnes, Nicholas, and ,Elizabeth Robinson. John Robinson, surety—July 13, 1796.

Carney, Charles, and Susannah Gish, dau. Jacob Gish—March 27, 1816.

Carney, Matthew, and Hannah Adams,—1788. (See below. Written Patrick in min. return.)

Carney, Patrick, and Susannah Hester—1787.

Carney, Patrick, and Hannah Adams. Matt Harvey, surety—Feb. 12, 1788.

Carpenter, Samuel, and Mary Persinger—Jan. 3, 1797.

Carpenter, Solomon, and Lucretia Prentice, dau. Daniel Prentice. Thomas Carpenter, surety—Sept. 5, 1783.

Carper, Benjamin, and Elizabeth Vanmeter —April 2, 1800.

Carper, Isaac, and Susannah Lovain. Abraham Lovain, surety—1797.

Carper, Jacob, and Mary Newell, dau. John Newell—April 3, 1814.

Carper, Jacob, and Elizabeth Nutter, dau. Zadock Nutter—May 24, 1815.

Carper, Jacob, and Sally Raymer—Jan. 5, 1796.

Carper, John, and Margaret Miller, dau. Valentine Miller—June 20, 1820.

Carroll, John, and Barbara Black, dau. Christian Black—May 15, 1812.

Carroll, Luke, and Elizabeth Black, dau. Frederick Black, dec.—Oct. 25, 1817.

Carroll, William, and Jinney Adams, dau. of "wife of Richard Wilson"—Dec. 29, 1789.

Carson, Alexander, and Mary Adams, dau. John Adams—Oct. 1, 1821.

Cartmill, Henry, and Elinor Cartmill. James Cartmill, surety—July 3, 1775.

Cartmill, Henry, and Sarah Anderson, dau. James Anderson, May 27, 1776.

Cartmill, Henry, and Mary Luney. Bartil Cartmill and John Luney, surety—July 3, 1786.

Cartmill, Henry, and Margaret Wallace, dau. David Wallace—Aug 27, 1788.

Cartmill, Henry, and Isabella Bogar—Feb. 4, 1799.

Carvin, Edward, and Nancy Persinger—Feb. 12, 1788.

Carvin, Edward, and Hannah Stover, dau.

William Stover—Jan. 22, 1812.

Casey, Hiram, and Elizabeth Goode, dau. George Goode—Oct. 29, 1821.

Casey, William, and Sarah Hudson. William Hudson, surety—Nov. 29, 1784.

Cassler, Thomas, and Catherine Myers, dau. Jacob Myers—Feb. 9, 1805.

Chapman, George, and Nancy Crawford, dau. Andrew Crawford, Sr.—Aug. 16, 1814.

Chapman, George, and Lucinda Wilson, dau. James Wilson—July 31, 1820.

Chapman, Thomas, and Polly Rife, dau. David Rife—March 16, 1812.

Chenowith, James Ruxton, and Rebecca Lassley—Aug. 20, 1799.

Chenowith, James, and Nancy Crawford, dau. William Crawford—Nov. 3, 1813.

Chenowith, Nicholas Ruxton, and Mary Switzer—April 12. 1790.

Cherry, James, and Elizabeth Greenwood, dau. Jane Greenwood—April 12, 1814.

Chitwood, Joshua, and Jane Robinson, dau. John Robinson—April 26, 1786.

Chivers, Andrew, and Rebecca Richardson, widow of Joel—Nov. 2, 1807.

Chrisman, Joseph, and Mary Gholson, dau. Anthony Gholson—Aug. 25, 1788.

Circle Andrew, Andrew, and Betsy Brookman, dau. John Brookman—Nov. 9, 1807.

Circle, John, and Margaret Nicely, dau. Jacob Nicely—Feb 17, 1817.

Circle, Lewis and Martha Lee Hooke, dau. Stephen Hooke—Dec. 15, 1812.

Circle, Manuel (aged 21y. 6m.), and Catherine Kemp. John Kemp, surety—July 23, 1803.

Circle, Peter, Jr., and Fanny Hively, dau. Jacob Hively—Nov. 27, 1807.

Clack, Henry, and Mary Shumaker. Peter Shumaker, surety—Feb. 2, 1792.

Clair, (see Clear) George, and Susannah Kessler—Jacob Bishop, surety—July 19, 1787.

Clancey, James, and Nancy Ochletree, dau. John Ochletree—April 15, 1788.

Clancey, William, and Betsy Anderson, dau. Joseph Anderson—April 3, 1783.

Clark, Amos, and Anne Duval. Cornelius Duval, surety—Feb. 12, 1786.

Clark, Christopher, and Agnes Wright, dau. Peter Wright—Nov. 9, 1787.

Clark, David (son of Michael and Elizabeth), and Rachel Anderson, dau. Curtis and Elizabeth Anderson—Jan. 17, 1788.

Clark, George, and Margaret Little, dau. William Little—Jan. 6, 1794.

Clark, George, and Ann Gharst, dau. Jacob Gharst—June 24, 1820.

Clark, John, and Nancy Martin, dau. Johnson Martin—Dec. 12, 1805.

Clark, John, and Polly Lockhart—Aug. 29, 1797.

Clark, Michael, and Nancy Hampton, dau. John Hampton—Feb. 7, 1809.

Clark, Samuel, and Rebecca Livingston, dau. Wm. Livingston—March 3, 1797.

Clark, Thomas, and Betsy Hampton, dau. John Hampton—July 7, 1814.

Clark, William, and Judith Hancock, dau. Col. George Hancock—Jan. 5, 1808.

Clear, (see Clore) Thomas, and Sarah Miller, dau. John Miller—May 20, 1794.

Clegg, Samuel, and Mary Stanback. Alexander Clegg, surety—Dec. 9, 1800.

Clerk, (see Clark) Samuel and Polly McCall, dau. John McCall, Sr.—July 31, 1810.

Clifton, Samuel, and Polly Tinsdall—Sept. 20, 1794.

Clore, Jacob, and Betsy Fringer, dau. Christopher Fringer—June 13, 1804.

Clore, Thomas, and Sarah Miller, dau. John Miller—May 20, 1794.

Cloyd, David (son, Michael and Elizabeth), and Rachel Anderson, dau. Curtis and Elizabeth Anderson—Jan. 17, 1788.

Cloyd, James, and Catherine Eagle—May 5, 1791.

Cloyd, John, and Mary Withrow, dau. William Withrow—Nov. 13, 1793.

Cloyd, Joseph, and Ann Brooks, dau. James Brooks—Nov. 2, 1805.

Cloyd, Joseph, and Sarah Bennett, dau. Moses Bennett—Oct. 12, 1803.

Cloyd, Michael, and Mary Bennett—May 16, 1797.

Cluck, Henry, and Mary Shumaker, dau. Peter Shumaker—1792.

Coffman, Joseph, and Anne Amen. Dirst Ferguson, surety—Dec. 12, 1795. Amen, surety—March 30. 1801.

Coin, Joseph, and Peggy Ferguson. Andrew Coke, Richard, and Mary Richie—1789.

Cole, John, and Catherine Bryan, dau. William Bryan—Sept. 4, 1786.

Cole, Richard, and Mary Richie, dau. Mary Gibson, Jan. 12, 1789.

Coleman, John, and Vina Knuckles, dau. John Knuckles—Jan. 29, 1791.

Combs, John, and Susan Etter, dau. Jacob Etter—Dec. 16. 1822.

Comby, Aquilla, and Elizabeth Riddle, dau. Andrew Riddle—Dec. 23, 1813.

Compton, William, and Mary Pate. Mathew Compton and Jeremiah Pate, surety— Jan. 13, 1797.

Compton, William, and Drucilla Wray. Joseph Wray, surety—Sept. 8, 1801.

Compton, William, and Jane Allen, dau. Hugh Allen—Oct. 21, 1811.

Connell, William, and Anna Peck, dau. John Peck—July 7, 1818.

Conner, Daniel, and Hannah McDonald—Jan. 15, 1786.

Conner, Dennis, and Sarah Fanning—Nov. 11, 1773.

Conner, Lawrence, and Margaret Bane—Feb. 3, 1783.

Conner, Terrance, and Anna Boone, dau. William Boone—Jan. 26, 1786.

Cook, George, and Rachel Bilbro, dau. William Bilbro, dec.—March 1, 1817.

Cook, Jeremiah, and Elizabeth Beckner, dau. Abraham Beckner—Aug. 31, 1820.

Cook, John, and Elizabeth Moyers, dau. George Moyers—May 12, 1818.

Cook, Joseph, and Elizabeth Lemmon, dau. George Lemmon—June 10, 1815.

Cook, Moses F., and Sally N. McClanahan, dau. William McClanahan—May 5, 1810.

Cook, William, and Barbara Hawbert, dau. George Hawbert—April 8, 1820.

Cook, Zacheriah, and Barbara Lemmon, dau. George Lemmon—Dec. 7, 1821.

Coon, Jacob, and Frances Jennings—Dec. 28, 1821.

Coon, John and Rachel Smith—Aug. 15, 1799.

Coon, John, and Elizabeth Epley, dau. John Epley—Oct. 30, 1804.

Coon, Michael, and Ellizabeth Huddle. George Huddle, surety—April 26, 1801.

Coon, Michael ("aged 21y, 6m"), and Elizabeth Kelly, dau. George Kelly—April 6, 1803.

Coon, Peter, and Margaret Beard—Feb. 22, 1799.

Coones, Matthew, and Mary Snodgrass—June 8, 1780. (Written Cooney on Min, ret.)

Cooper, Alexander, and Sally Sheets, dau. Jacob Sheets—July 26, 1812.

Cooper, Edmund, and Catherine Mason, 'both over 21"—Sept. 7, 1797.

Cooper, John, and Margaret Richardson, dau. Robert Richardson—May 23, 1821.

Cooper, John, and Mary Ann Hannon, dau. Samuel Hannon—Aug. 11, 1821.

Cooper, William, and Polly Boughman. Henry Baughman, surety—Nov. 29, 1801.

Copeland, Charles, and Henningham Bernerd, dau. John Bernard—Oct. 13, 1808.

Copp, George, and Christine Critz, dau. George Critz, dec.—Oct. 22, 1805.

Cornell, William, and Elizabeth Rankin—

Jan. 2, 1802.

Cornelius, James, and Martha Bandy—May 3, 1799.

Cosby, William, and Mary Rowe, dau. James Rowe—Sept. 19, 1807.

Coulter, Nelson, and Polly Thompson—Feb. 25, 1813.

Cowden, James, and Sarah Hawkins—July 4, 1775.

Cox, Abner, and Mary Rutherford, dau. Halsard Rutherford—March 26, 1821.

Cox, Allen, and Margaret Davis—Dec. 20, 1791.

Cox, Ezekiel, and Elizabeth All, dau Elinor Nell) All—May 20, 1790.

Cox, James, and Catherine Neely, dau. Jacob Neely—Oct. 9, 1820.

Cox, John, and Rebecca Dunn. Wm. Cox, surety—July 28, 1780.

Crabb, Francis T., and Elizabeth H. Mitchell, dau. Edward Mitchell—Sept. 2, 1808.

Craft, Daniel, and Betsy Camper, dau. Peter Camper—Dec. 31, 1807.

Craft, Daniel, and Mary Hamilton, dau. John Hamilton—June 29, 1814.

Craft, David, and Polly Lypes, dau. Moses Lypes—Nov. 4, 1821.

Craft, George, and Mary Critz—Nov. 13, 1799.

Craft, Jacob, and Catherine Zimmerman, dau. Andrew Zimmerman—Feb. 12, 1821.

Craft, James, and Sophia Wayman, dau. John Wayman, Dec. 2, 1813.

Craft, John, and Lucy Camper. John Camper, surety—March 11, 1799.

Craft, Jonathan, and Barbery Hart, dau. George Hart—Nov. 13, 1815.

Craft, Philip, and Elizabeth Rhinehart, June 14, 1821.

Craft, William, and Maria Niece, dau. Jacob Niece—Feb. 22, 1821.

Craig, John, and Ally Todd, dau. Samuel—Jan. 11, 1792.

Crawford, Alexander, and Elizabeth McClure, dau. Samuel McClure—1794.

Crawford, Alexander, and, Polly Carper, dau. Jacob Carper—Sept. 27, 1820.

Crawford Andrew, and Euphus Batey—Nov. 23, 1788.

Crawford, Andrew, and Jane Weirs, dau. James Weirs—Nov. 23, 1814.

Crawford, English, and Mary Caldwell. Hugh Caldwell, surety—June 17, 1793.

Craword, James, and Jeanne McClellan—April 4, 1799.

Crawford, James, and Jean Poage, dau. Jean Poage, senr."—Sept. 5, 1791.

Crawford, James, and Sarah Vansant, dau.

Isiah Vansant—Oct. 21, 1786.

Crawford, James, and Elinor Hunter (mar. return says HENSTED), "of lawful age"— Feb. 20, 1797.

Crawford, John, and Jenny Read, widow of William Read—April 26, 1809.

Crawford, John, and Elizabeth Hamilton, widow of John Hamilton—June 9, 1812.

Crawford, John, and Mary Weiss, dau. James Weiss—Oct. 6, 1812.

Crawford, Nimrod, and Elizabeth Gray, dau. James Gray—Aug. 19, 1794.

Crawford, Robert, and Elizabeth Crawford, dau. James Crawford—Feb. 22, 1822.

Crawford, Samuel, and Mary Switzer, dau. John Switzer—Nov. 2, 1816.

Crawford, Samuel, and Polly Duddin (21y)— July 27, 1798.

Crawford, Samuel, and Jane Mason, March 23, 1771.

Crawford, Thomas, and Ann McNeely, dau. William McNeely—April 13, 1790.

Crawford, Thomas, and Rachel Dodd, dau. Joseph Dodd, dec.—Aug. 3, 1819.

Crawford, William, and Martha Cooper— June 15, 1786.

Crawford, William, and Sarah Galloway, dau. Benjamin Galloway—Aug. 20, 1804.

Crawford, William, and Susanne Dabney— 1781.

Cress, Gearge, and Catherine Frantz, dau. Christopher Frantz—June 18, 1809.

Cribbers, Thomas, and Nancy Guthrie—Oct. 9, 1787.

Crider, Jacob, and Catherine Haynes, May— 1786.

Crider, Peter, and Catherine Crush, Peter Crush, surety—Jan. 7, 1798.

Crill, William, and Catherine Frantz, dau. Peter Frantz—April 19, 1816.

Crist, George, and Elizabeth Wilson, dau. James Wilson—Jan. 21, 1820.

Critz, Conrad, and Barbara Critz, dau. Nicholas Critz—March 21, 1798.

Crockett, Charles Lewis, and Hary Harrison Boyer, dau. Henry Boyer—Nov. 4, 1822.

Croiden, Henry, and Mary Baugh, widow of Manley Baugh—Dec. 31, 1821.

Cross, John, and Polly Mays, dau. John Mays —1795.

Cross, Thomas and Elizabeth Alderson, dau. Curtis Alderson—Dec. 29, 1801.

Cross, William, and Ann Allen, widow of Hugh Allen—April 19, 1820.

Cross, William, and Mary Eliza Rice, dau. John Rice—Sept. 16, 1794.

Crow, John, and Wilima Phipps. Joshua

Phipps, surety—Feb. 13, 1787.

Crow, Mathias, and Elizabeth Armstrong. Robt. Armstrong, surety—Feb. 16, 1801.

Crowl, Henry, and Elizabeth McLaughlin, widow of Charles McLaughlin—Jan. 6, 1819.

Crump, Fendall, and Elizabeth Griffith, dau. John Griffith—Sept. 17, 1803.

Crumpecker, Benjamin, and Polly Stoner, June 25, 1822.

Crumpecker, John, anl Mary Gish, widow of John Gish—Dec. 21, 1821.

Crush, Henry, and Nancy Coulter. Samuel Coulter, surety—Aug. 31, 1803.

Crush, Jacob, and Susanna Swisher, dau. Mathias Swisher—Jan. 18, 1821.

Crush, James, and Susanna Coulter, dau. Samuel Coulter—April 4, 1816.

Crush, Peter, and Elizabeth Williams, widow of Lewis Williams—Jan. 15, 1820.

Crush, William, and Polly Inglehart, dau. George Inglehart—Dec. 15 1808.

Crutchfield, John, and Lucinda Tawnes, dau. Adam Tawnes—Jan. 11, 1821.

Crutchfield, John, and Elizabeth Draper, dau. Benjamin Draper—Nov. 15, 1820.

Crutchfield, James, and Sally Cleage, dau. Samuel Cleage (James son of Robert)— June 19, 1820.

Culman, Michael, and Ann Pitzer—Oct. 14, 1783.

Cummerferd, Patrick, and Frances Franklin, dau. Frances Franklin—July 28, 1812.

Cummings, Absolum, and Rebecca Stone, dau. John Stone—Feb. 21, 1816.

Cummings, Seth, and Mary Magdalene Spessard, dau. Henry Spessard—Oct. 3, 1820.

Cunningham, John, and Polly Newman, dau. John Newman—June 1, 1817.

Cunningham, William, and Nancy Newman, dau. James Newman—May 28, 1821.

Cunningham, William, and Catherine Hartman, dau. George Hartman—Oct. 6, 1819.

Cunningham, William, and Sarah Walker, dau. John Walker—May 15, 1810.

Cunninfham, William, and Elizabeth Solomon—Nov. 30, 1810.

Cups, Jacob, and Eve Kilmer, dau. George Kilmer—Oct. 30, 1810.

Curry, John (son of William), and Margaret Adams, dau. William Adams—Sept. 25, 1777.

Custard, Adam, and Margaret Gross, dau. Martin Gross, dec.—March 6, 1811.

Custard, Isaac, and Rachell Cop, dau. Christian Copp—July 25, 1795.

Custard, Jacob, and Susannah Lypes, dau.

Moses Lypes—Nov. 8, 1820.

Custard, John, and Polly Smiley, dau. James Smiley, dec.—Sept. 10, 1809.

Custard, John, and Mary Biglar, dau. Mark Biglar—Jan. 28, 1806.

Custard, Joseph, and Martha Cleage, dau. Alexander Cleage—Jan. 15, 1811.

Custer, George, and Hetty Pertyfield, dau. Peter Pertyfield ("living in Holstein")—Sept. 19, 1810.

Custer, George, and Peggy Myers, son of George Custer, Sr., dau. Jacob Myers—Dec. 15, 1798.

—D—

Dagger, Peter, and Mary Solomon—March 22, 1794.

Dame, David, and Margaret Cripser, dau. Mathias Cripser—Oct. 30, 1802.

Dame, Jacob, and Elizabeth Killenger, dau. Randolph Killinger—July 23, 1810.

Damewood, Henry, and Leanna Smyth—July 24, 1799.

Damewood, James, and Mary Huffman, dau. Jacob Huffman—March 26, 1803.

Damron, John, and Molly Hardy. Thomas Hardy, surety—May 23, 1796.

Daniel, John, and Judith Brafford—May 7, 1808.

Darby, James, and Polly Simmons, dau. Joseph and Aggatha Simmons—Jan. 24, 1798.

Darnel, Stephen, and Esther Livingston. John Livingston, surety—Jan. 30, 1796.

Darr, George, and Polly M'Gowen, widow Robert M'Gowen—April 8, 1806.

Darr, John, and Mary Franklin—May 21, 1800.

Darr, John, and Alny Ruthford—June 11, 1812.

Darr, Joseph, and Elizabeth Groves, widow John Groves—March 14, 1806.

Daugherty, Daniel, and Charity Thompson—July 21, 1786.

Dougherty, James, and Elizabeth Hamilton, dau. James Hamilton—May 21, 1796.

Daugherty, John, and Adicey Elder, "stepdau. of Wm. Guthry")—Sept. 7, 1789.

Daugherty, William, and Mary Scantland. James Scantland, surety—Dec. 21, 1788.

Daugherty, William, and Mary Bridger—Jan. 20, 1786.

Davidson, Robert, and Sally Davidson, dau. William Davidson—Jan. 1, 1801.

Davis, Alexander, and Clora Speckhart, dau. Henry Speckhart—May 16, 1807.

Davis, James, and Betsy Snodgrass—June 30, 1801.

Davis, Silas, and Elizabeth Phillips, dau. Samuel Phillips—May 23, 1793.

Davis, Thomas, and Mary Lauthron, "widow Lawhorn" consent—Feb. 1, 1780.

Davis, William, and Hannah Trotter—May 20, 1778.

Davis, William, and Sarah Trotter—Aug. 28, 1778.

Davis, William, and Elizabeth Plymell—Oct. 19, 1791.

Dawson, Samuel G. and Maria Barnwell—Jan. 25, 1816.

Day, John, and Polly Richardson, dau. Jacob Richardson—April 4, 1804.

Day, Samuel, and Eleanor Bannister. Francis Bannister, surety—Dec. 26, 1801.

Deacon, William, and Ann Lewill, dau.-Thomas Lewill—April 18, 1809.

Deal, Peter, and Mary Stover, dau. George Stover—Sept. 18, 1811.

Deal, Robert, and Mary Moore, dau. James Moore—May 6, 1803.

Deal, Samuel, and Mary Brewbaker, dau. Abraham Brewbaker, dec.—April 11, 1814.

Deardorf, Jacob, and Sarah Stiley, dau. Jacob Stiley, dec.—April 26, 1808.

Deardorf, John, and Catherine Hirshbarger, dau. Christopher Hirshbarger—Feb. 7, 1804.

Deaton, John, and Jane Baker, dau. Robert Baker, dec—May 21, 1812.

Deaton, Nathan, and Sally Mitchell, dau. John Mitchell—June 1, 1819.

Deeds, Valentine, and Catherine Brookman, dau. John Brookman—March 4, 1811.

Defore, John, and Frances Fatham. John Fatham, surety—Nov. 2, 1784.

Delbridge, Robert, and Nancy Haney—June 10, 1788. "dau.-in-law of ....Beau," surety.

Delbridge, Robert, and Elizabeth Fisher—July 9, 1799.

Dempsey, Absolum, and Elizabeth Bolton, dau. Henry Bolton—Oct. 20, 1809.

Dempsey, Dubartis, and Mary Alfriend—Jan. 5, 1813.

Dempsey, Hugh, and Catherine Belinger, dau. John Belinger—Aug. 25, 1809.

Dempsey, John, and Rachel Solomon—Sept. 5, 1788.

Dempsey, Mark, and Mary Turner. Consent by Wm. Dempsey and James Turner—Aug. 23, 1788.

Dennis, John Henry, and Susanna Mitchell, dau. Edward Mitchell—May 27, 1815.

Dennis, Joseph, and Anna Bibee, dau. John and Elizabeth Bibee—Dec. 22, 1792.

Denny, Daniel, and Elizabeth Gray—Aug. 19,

1797.

Dent, John, and Rachel Kesler, dau. Christopher Kesler—Jan. 23, 1794.

Denton, Benjamin, and Peggy Anderson, dau. Robert Anderson—July 22, 1793.

Denton, John, and Anne Solonbarger—Oct. 11, 1814.

Depew, Elijah, and Elizabeth Peck, dau. Banj. Peck—May 27, 1794.

Depew, Isaac, and Jane Jones. Consent by Elizabeth Jones—Jan. 19, 1780.

Depew, Jacob, and Mary Peck, dau. Benjamin Peck—July 19, 1796.

Depew, James, and Margaret Peck. Adam Peck, surety—May 8, 1788.

Depew, John, and Mary Seagraves, dau. Samuel Seagraves—Oct. 2, 1792.

Depew, Samuel, and Mary Dean. Consent by guardian, Col. Hugh Rose—March 7, 1787.

Derman, John, and Ann Lewill, dau. Thomas Lewill—April 18, 1809.

Derrick, Michael, and Elizabeth Moyer, dau. Jacob Moyer—June 16, 1789.

Detzel, Thomas, and Letricia Depew, dau. John Depew—Nov. 13, 1787.

Dewall, Cornelius, and Ann Pryor, dau. Joseph Pryor—May 8, 1788.

Dewese, David, and Jane Harry, dau. Evan Harry—Nov. 23, 1787.

Deyerle, Charles, and Mary Poage, dau. Jean Poage—Oct. 18, 1797.

Deyerle, Joseph, and Ann Crawford, dau. James Crawford—Aug. 1, 1820.

Dickenson, Adam, and Elizabeth Kyle, dau. Barclay Kyle—Oct. 16, 1821.

Dickenson, John, Charlotte Kyle, dau. William Kyle—Dec. 8, 1809.

Dickey, Andrew L., and Elizabeth Gurtner. dau. Philip Gurtner, dec.—Sept. 29, 1818.

Dickey, James, and Elizabeth Steel, dau. George Steel—Nov. 16, 1815.

Dickey, Robert L., and Margaret Nace, dau. John Nace—March 27, 1817.

Diesher, John, and Susanna Sheets—Nov. 28, 1794. Jacob Sheets, surety.

Disher, Christian, and Frances Circle, dau Peter Circle—Feb. 28, 1816.

Disher, Daniel, and Susannah Sheets, dau. Jacob Sheets, dec.—Dec. 15, 1808.

Disher, Jacob B., and Christina Rule, dau. George Rule—Aug. 4, 1806.

Disher, Peter, and Polly Sheets, dau. Jacob Sheets—March 16, 1806.

Dill, Andrew, and Mary Cross, dau. John Cross—May 24, 1821.

Dilman, Abram, and Elizabeth Hypes, dau. John Hypes—Sept. 29, 1819.

Dilman, Daniel, and Mary Dill, dau. Henry Dill—Dec. 22, 1814.

Dilman, Jacob, and Elizabeth Burk—Aug. 12, 1806.

Dilman, Michael, and Susanna Hypes, dau. John Hypes—Nov. 26, 1821.

Dishman, J. . . . . . ., and Jane Gunn. William Gunn, surety—July 25, 1788.

Dirjin-Durgin-Durjan.

Dirgin, Barney, and Nancy Knox, dau. Elixha Knox, Sr.—Aug. 26, 1799.

Dirgin. John, and Elizabeth Hewit, dau. Patrick Hewit—Nov. 2, 1790.

Dixon, John, and Rachel Howard—May 8, 1787.

Dodge, Hezekiah, and Granville Haynes, dau. Joseph Haynes, dec.—April 5, 1819.

Dodd, Aaron, and Effey Crawford, dau. William Crawford—July 7, 1811.

Dodd, John, and Sarah Stone, dau. John Stone—Feb. 3, 1812.

Dodd, William, and Mary Price (Pierce in Min ret.)—Aug. 31, 1782.

Dodd, William, and Elizabeth Leffel, dau. John Laffel, dec.—Sept. 15, 1807.

Donahammer, George, and Maagaret Delong. George Delong, surety—March 8, 1803.

Donaho, Edward, and Susannah Mitchell (over 21), late of Montgomery Co.—Aug. 15, 1803.

Donoho, James, and Margaret Reyburn. James Reyburn, surety—Feb. 18, 1785.

Donavan, Cornelius, and Martha Snodgrass, dau. James Snodgrass—April 28, 1792.

Donner, Michael, and Catherine Coon, dau. Michael Coon—April 9, 1805.

Doosing, John and Elesander McClure. Wm. McClure, surety—April 24, 1820.

Douglas, John, and Ann Morris, dau. Richard Morris—June 23, 1788.

Downey, Michael, and Mary Persinger—June 26, 1789.

Drais, Jacob, and Agnes Mankipile, dau. Michael Mankipile—Aug. 15, 1804.

Drake, Zacheriah, and Rhoda Neely, dau. John Neely, esquire—Jan. 13, 1804.

Draper, Benjamin, and Paisilly Katen (Kalen)—Dec. 8, 1800.

Draper, Thomas and Siller Breede—Aug. 4, 1780.

Dressler, Peter (son Harry), and Barbara Mallow, dau. Michael Mallow—June 28, 1806.

Drummond, Thomas, and Betsy Biggs, widow William Biggs—Jan. 9, 1812.

Dudding, John, and Sarah Bellamy—Feb. 15, 1792.

Dudding, John, and Rebeckah Persinger, dau. Christopher Persinger—Nov. 12, 1804.

Duff, Isiah, and Margaret Skeen, dau. Joseph Skeen—Oct. 11, 1811.

Dunbar, William, and Sarah Bridgeland— Oct. 12, 1815.

Dunbar, William, and Cynthia Dijarnett, dau. Richard—Dec. 28, 1819.

Duncan, George, and Levina Weirs. James Weirs, surety—Dec. 30, 1796.

Duncan, John, and Ann Morris. Richard Morris, surety—1788.

Duncan, Robert, and Catherine Darr, dau. Joseph Darr—Oct. 18, 1804.

Dunlop, Robert, and Susanna Jones, dau. Allen Jones—Jan. 22, 1816.

Dwyer, John, and Susanna Deeds, dau. Peter Deeds—Jan. 9, 1816.

Dysher, Peter, and Sally Moyers—Jan. 2, 1799.

—E—

Eads, John, and Sarah West, dau. John West —Feb. 26, 1790.

Eads, Thomas, and Pricilla West. John West, surety—Aug. 3, 1787.

Eads, William, and Jane Gillespy. William Gillspy (a brother), surety—July 10, 1797.

Eager, James, and Judith Breedlove—Oct. 10, 1792.

Eager, John, and Ufus Crawford, dau. John Crawford—Nov. 2, 1791.

Eakin, Henry, and Feby Garst, dau. Jacob Garst—Dec. 3, 1811.

Eakin, Robert, and Mary Martin—Feb. 5, 1778.

Eakin, Thomas, and Polly Walker—June 11, 1779.

Eakin, Thomas, and Mary Caldwell, dau. Willima Caldwell—Feb. 6, 1816.

Eakin, William, and Viranda Ripley, dau. James Ripley, dec—July 24, 1816.

Eakin, William, and Betty Ann Welch, dau. James Welch—Sept. 30, 1811.

Eakin, William, and Rebecca Cummings, dau. William Cummings—Aug. 16, 1816.

Early, James, and Mary Broadwater, dau. Charles Broadwater—March 18, 1807.

Eason, Samuel, and Anne Goodson—Feb. 12, 1779.

Eath, Michael, and Barbara Hess (Eath?)— July 25, 1797.

Echols, Henry, and Catherine Kessler, dau. John Kessler—June 25, 1807.

Echolds, Joseph, and Magdalene Gharst, dau. Frederick Gharst—Dec. 10, 1805.

Eddy, James, and Elizabeth Zimmerman,

dau. Andrew Zimmerman—Sept. 4, 1820.

Edington, Philip, and Catherine Day. Evan Day, surety—Dec. 14, 1797.

Edington, Philip, and Mary A. Watson—Sept. 27, 1819.

Edminston, William, and Janett Wilson, dau. Mary Wilson—April 9, 1799.

Edwards, John, and Barbara Faught, dau. Gasper Faught—July 4, 1785.

Edwards, John, and Betsy Stevens—April 15, 1789.

Eller, John, and Catherine Brubaker, dau John Brubaker—Feb 10, 1818.

Elliott, John, and Margaret Fizer, dau. Adam Fizer—March 6, 1816.

Elliott, John, and Jane Cross. William Cross, surety—Oct. 1, 1785.

Elliott, William, and Isabella Morris, dau. Richard Morris—Oct. 11, 1790.

Elmore, Andrew, and Sophia Huffman, dau. Jacob Huffman—Sept. 1, 1813.

Elmore, John, and Catherine Kilmore, dau. George Kilmore—May 29, 1820.

Elmore, William, and Hannah Huffman, dau. Jacob Huffman—July 22, 1811.

Emerick, George, and Catherine Cesslor (Ceptor?), dau. Thomas—May 3, 1796.

Enders, Adam, and Jean Hart—Sept. 7, 1790.

Enders, Adam, and Susy Scott—Oct. 2, 1810.

English (Ingles?), Crockett, and Emeline M. Lewis, dau. Andrew Lewis, dec.—June 5, 1821.

Entsminger, Henry, and Rebecca Ellender— Oct 19, 1791.

Erlizer, Henry, and Betsy Idle. Martin Idle, surety—Nov. 8, 1798.

Ervin, John, and Margaret Wysong, dau. Fiatt Wysong—Jan. 24, 1799.

Etzler, John, and Mary Magdalene Peters, dau. Jacob Peters—April 16, 1815.

Etter, George, and Elizabeth Wax, dau. Henry Wax—March 9, 1791.

Etter, Michael, and Anna Pefley, dau. David Pefley—Sept. 18, 1820.

Eubank, Moses, and Nancy Overstreet, dau. William Overstreet—June 10, 1812.

Evans, William, and Betsy Spessard, dau. Michael Spessard—Feb. 4, 1812.

—F—

Falls, James, and Sarah Switzer, dau. William Switzer, dec.—Dec. 23, 1813.

Falls, John, and Margaret Hogans. James Switzer, surety—July 6, 1822.

Falls, John, and Lydia Camper, dau. Solomon Camper—Sept. 17, 1804.

Falls, Joseph, and Peggy Fink, dau. Daniel

Fink—Nov. 27, 1804.

Falls, Peter, and Elizabeth Hoover, dau. Peter Hoover—Aug. 15, 1815.

Farrar, Dr. A. D., and Anne McFerran—Nov. 14, 1822.

Farrier, Jacob, and Elizabeth Reynolds—June 7, 1799.

Farrier, William, and Sarah Caldwell, dau. John Caldwell—March 3, 1801.

Farrier, William, and Jane Kilpatrick—March 26, 1891.

Farris, Benjamin, and Amelia L. Baldwin, dau. George Baldwin—Dec. 31, 1822.

Farrow, Adam, and Catherine Grand—Oct. 16, 1805.

Farrow, Jacob, and Hannah Wolfinbarger, dau. Peter Wolfenbarger—Sept. 16, 1805.

Fascher, Daniel, and Murelas Eagle—Oct. 24, 1785.

Fasher, Michael, and Sarah Varner (over 21) Geo. Varner, brother, surety—May 5, 1802.

Faught, George, and Mary Persinger, dau. Christopher Persinger—Sept. 11, 1789.

Faught, John, and Jane Stull, dau. Sharlott Stull—April 7, 1794.

Feathers, Peter, and Susanna Bandy, dau. Richard Bandy—Sept. 14, 1813.

Feller, Lawrence, and Catherine Hiner, widow of Peter Hiner, dec.—Dec. 2, 1805.

Ferguson, David, and Polly Sloan, dau. Archabald Sloan—May 25, 1804.

Ferguson, William, and Mary Burns, dau. John Burns—Jan. 12, 1819.

Ferrell, Abner, and Sarah Bilbro. William Bilbro of Bedford, surety—Jan. 1798.

Ferrell, David, and Elizabeth Smith, dau. Jacob Smith—Feb. 23, 1822.

Ferrell, John, and Barbara Niswonger (over 21), dau. John—Nov. 24, 1794.

Ferrell, Stephen, and Nancy Tosh—Nov. 28, 1797.

Fields, Richard, and Fanny Russell—Feb. 14, 1804.

Fife, Edward, and Catherine Roberts (23)—Aug. 10, 1797.

Figgitt, Henry, and Susanna Smith, dau. William Smith—May 26, 1821.

Figgitt, Thomas S. and Jane Gray, dau. William Gray—March 16, 1822.

Filson, Robert, and Sarah Hudson—Nov. 17, 1796.

Filson, Robert, and Jenny McNeel, dau. Daniel McNeel—June 16, 1806.

Finney, John, and Rachel Taylor, dau. Jonathan Taylor—Sept. 18, 1787.

Finney, Pleasant, and Susanna Manspile, dau. Thomas Manspile—March 20, 1804.

Firestone, John, and Peggy Thresher, dau. Christopher Thresher—Aug. 1, 1803.

Firestone, Matthias, and Mary Hill, dau. James and Sarah Hill—Nov. 3, 1798.

Fisher, Aaron, and Dorothea Obenchain, dau Philip Obenchain—Nov. 11, 1822.

Fisher, Jacob, and Sarah Piffley, dau. Samuel Piffley—Nov. 5, 1821.

Fisher, James, and Nancy Ovenchain, dau. Philip Ovenchain—March 23, 1818.

Fisher, John, and Elizabeth Graybill, dau. John Graybill—May 20, 1811.

Fisk, Henry, and Martha Wiley. John Wiley, surety—Jan. 30, 1795.

Fizer, Samuel, and Sarah Spangler, dau. Charles Spangler—March 13, 1816.

Flanagan, David, and Lucy Peary—Sept. 9, 1800.

Flarity Flarherty.

Flarety, Adam, and Harriet Lavender, dau. Robert Lavender—Dec. 27, 1807.

Fleming, William, and Sarah Lewis, dau. William Lewis—an. 29, 1818.

Fleshart, Francis, and Elizabeth Wysong, dau. Fyatt Wysong—Jan. 6, 1794.

Flesher, Conrad, and Elisabeth Lemmon, dau. Frederick Lemmon—July 19, 1802.

Flint, John, and Florence Wood, dau. Samuel Wood—Jan. 21, 1806.

Florah, James, and Barbara Helmintoller, dau. C. Helmintoller, dec.—Sept. 15, 1817.

Floyd, John, and Polly Querry, dau. Elijah Querry—April 14, 1813.

Fluqua, William, and Nancy Kelly—Nov. 16, 1809.

Flurnoy, Bird, and Susanna Amyx, dau. Same Amyx—May 5, 1818.

Fogg, James, and Martha Lefon, dau. Frances Lefon—Sept. 14, 1816.

Ford, Thomas, and Phebe Jones—Nov. 15, 1803.

Forrest, James, and Mazy Gardner, dau. Giles Gardner, dec.—March 11, 1805.

Forrester, David, and Elizabeth Ham, dau. Judy Lorton—Jan. 3, 1789.

Foster, Nathan, and Elizabeth Pitzezr. Jons Pitzer, surety—Nov. 18, 1795.

Foutt, Emanuel, and Betsy Zimmerman, dau. William Zimmerman—Dec. 22, 1818.

Foutz, Jihn, and Sally Persinger, dau. John Persinger—Dec. 3, 1819.

Foutz, John, and Elizabeth Spickart, dau. Henry Spickart—March 14, 1819.

Fowler, Elijah, and Anne Guthrie, dau. John Guthrie—Nov. 4. 1795.

Fox, Benjamin, and Elizabeth Anderson. Bartlett Anderson, surety—Aug. 20, 1799.

Francis, Abraham, and Phebe Taylor, dau. Jacob Taylor—Dec. 3, 1817.

Francis, Jacob, and Winafred Adams, dau. Henry Adams—May 20, 1804.

Francis, James, and Susanna Spickart, dau. Philip Spickart—March 17, 1814.

Francis, Joseph, and Elizabeth Haynes, dau. Benjamin Haynes—Jan. 7, 1807.

Francisco, Lewis, and Elizabeth Summerfield. Richard Summerfield, surety—Dec. 17, 1802.

Frankenbarger, Samuel, and Elizabeth Harshbarger—Nov. 1, 1808.

Franklin, Elijah, and Nancy Gorman—Jan. 10, 1821.

Franklin, James, and Catherine Stover, dau. William Stover—March 16, 1806.

Franklin, John, and Rachle Crist, dau. Philip Crist—Aug. 4, 1812.

Franklin, Nathan, and Elizabeth Litton, widow of Wm. Litton—March 14, 1804.

Franklin, Peter, and Polly Lark, dau. John Lark—Oct. 29, 1821.

Frantz, Henry, and Anna Keagy, dau. Henry Keagy—Nov. 8, 1819.

Frantz, Henry, and Catherine Nofsinger, dau. David Nofsinger—March 26, 1821.

Frantz, Isaac, and Catherine Circle, dau. Peter Circle—March 6, 1817.

Frantz, John H., and Mary M'Cully, dau. Joseph M'Cully—Feb. 19, 1818.

Frantz, John, and Esther Stover, dau. William Stover—Aug. 17, 1810.

Frantz, John, and Betsy Persinger, dau. John Persinger—June 16, 1807.

Frantz, Michael, and Elizabeth Kish, dau. Christian Kish—Nov. 23, 1802.

Frazier, Luke, and Sarah Jordon—Dec. 25, 1792.

Freeman, William, and Betsy Baggs—Sept. 15, 1798.

French, Thomas, and Sarah Johnson. William W. Johnson, surety—Oct. 6, 1812.

Friary, Adam, and Elizabeth Dingledine, dau Baker Dingledine—Dec. 18, 1819.

Fringer, Christopher, and Susanna Zirkle— Dec. 5, 1787.

Fry, Matthias, and Elizabeth Armstrong. Thomas Armstrong, surety—March 10, 1801.

Fudge, Conrad, and Elizabeth Persinger. Jacob Persinger, surety—May 20, 1798.

Fulheart, John, and Mary France, dau. Peter France—Feb. 28, 1816.

Fulton, David, and Martha Snodgrass, dau. William Snodgrass—May 23, 1791.

Fulton, James, and Sarah Whitley—March 23, 1772.

Fultz (see Foutz).

—G—

Gamble, Robert, Jr. (of Richmond), and Letitia Breckenridge, dau. James Breckenridge—June. 2, 1807.

Gammon, Richard, and Sarah Gamble, "upwards 21." Parents dead—Nov. 23, 1781.

Ganby, Martin, and Caty Nininger, dau. Christian Niniger—March 22, 1820.

Gant, Joseph, and Mary Caldwell. Consent by Rachel Gant and Mary Caldwell—1793.

Gardner, John, and Sarah Nutter, dau. Zadok Nutter—June 7, 1817.

Garmon, Jacob, and Catherine Graybill. John Graybill, surety—Aug. 11, 1797.

Garmon, John, and Susanna Beckner. Howard Beckner, surety—1791.

Garmon, Patrick, and Frances Trotter—1788.

Garmon, Peter, and Christinah Horton, dau. Jacob Garfield—May 6, 1801.

Garnes, Benjamin Tapling, and Elizabeth Scantling, dau. Keene Scantling—Jan. 27, 1813.

Garnettson, John, and Rebekah Duncan. Jeremiah Duncan, surety—May 9, 1795.

Garwood, Joseph, and Martha McClellon. John McClellon, surety—Jan. 30, 1786.

Garwood, Samuel, and Mary Smiley. James Smiley, surety—March 12, 1820.

Gasburn, Frederick, and Mary Persinger, dau. Andrew Persinger—Nov. 14, 1820.

Gatewood, Warwick, and Margaret Beale, dau. Charles Beale—Sept. 16, 1822.

Gaunt, James, and Jane McCartney, widow— Sept 25, 1821.

Gay, John, and Sophia Mitchell, dau. Rev. Edward Mitchell—Oct. 5, 1813.

George, William, and Elinor Snodgrass—Feb. 9, 1779.

German, John, and Susanna Beckner—Oct. 10, 1791.

Gesset, Jehu, and Mary Noftzinger, dau. Jacob Noftzinger—Dec. 6, 1806.

Gharst, Frederick, Jr., and Lunnar Eller, dau. Jacob Eller—Dec. 29, 1809.

Gharst, Jacob, and Eve Minter, dau. Chris. Minter—Dec. 3, 1805.

Gharst, Jacob, and Fanny Richardson, dau. Robert Richardson—March 24, 1821.

Gharst, Jacob, and Polly Shaver, dau. Andrew Shaver—Nov. 13, 1820.

Gharst, John, and Tency Peffley, dau. David Peffley—March 3, 1821.

Ghaut, Abraham, and Katherine Ribble— March 17, 1801.

Gholson, John (son of Anthony), and Lucretla Griffith. Anthony Gholson, and John Griffith, surety—March 3, 1794.

Gholson, William, and Mary Cross. William Cross, surety—Dec. 9, 1784.

Gibson, Samuel, and Peggy Hannah, dau. Alexander Hannah—June 24, 1794.

Gifford, John, and Elizabeth Hugh—Jan. 15, 1781.

Gilkinson, Will, and Jane McMullin. Matt McMullin, surety—Dec. 22, 1794.

Gill, Edward, and Elizabeth Bails, dau. Ellis Bails—March 20, 1789.

Gill, John, and Elizabeth Duke, dau. John Duke—Oct. 14, 1818.

Gillespie, Gillespy, etc.

Gillespie, James, and Elizabeth Gillespie. Robert Gillespie, surety—July 29, 1779.

Gillespie, James, and Nancy H. Franklin, dau. Edmund Franklin—March2, 1822.

Gillespie, John, and Mary Thompson,, dau. William Thompson—July 30, 1792.

Gillespie, John (son of Simon and Rebecca), and Jane Harvey—Aug. 31, 1779.

Gillespie, John (son of James and Elizabeth), and Jane Harvey, dau. Robert Harvey—July 29, 1779

Gillespie, Robert, and Margaret Cole, dau John Cole—Aug. 11 1819.

Gillespie, Simon, and Juliet Grinville Halloway, dau. John Halloway—April 14, 1817.

Gillespie, William, and Sarah (Mary) Carpenter—May 24, 1780.

Gilliford, John, and Elizabeth Deardorf. Paul Deardorf, surety—March 18, 1805.

Gilliland, James, and Polly Karnes, dau. Jacob Karnes—Aug. 8, 1812.

Gilliland, John, and Peggy Paxton—Sept. 30, 1797.

Gilliland, John, and Sarah Walker. Henry Walker, surety—April 2, 1804.

Gilliland, Samuel, and Mary G. Haynes. Joseph Haynes, surety—Jan. 28, 1800.

Gillahand, Shepherd, and Jennet Harriet Haynes, dau. Joseph Haynes—Aug. 5, 1811.

Gilmon, Joseph, and Milly Rowland, dau. Capt. Thomas Rowland—Nov. 19, 1805

Gilmore, Hugh, and Lucretia Reynolds, dau. Hannah Reynolds—June 24, 1794.

Gilmore, John, and Magdaline Shepherd. Dubartis Shepherd, surety—June 7, 1791.

Gish, Abraham, and Esther Houtts, dau. John Houtts—Oct. 30, 1813.

Gish, Abraham, and Polly Fry, dau. Matthias Frye—June 1, 1805.

Gish, Christian, and Elizabeth Houtz, dau. John Houtz—Oct. 24, 1816.

Gish, Christian, and Susanna Neff, dau. John

Neff, Sr.—May 25, 1802.

Gish, Christian, and Mary McNeil. John McNeil, surety—Aug. 3, 1819.

Gish, David, and Lydia Eddington, dau. Philip Eldington. Sept. 15, 1821.

Gish, George, and Ruth Howell. Abner Howell, surety—July 15, 1809.

Gish, George, and Eliza Garman, dau. John Garman, dec.—June 8, 1818.

Gish, Jacob, and Rebecca Harshbarger, dau. Christian Harshbarger—March 9, 1816.

Cish, Jacob, and Mary Howell. Abner Howell, suretv—May 26, 1807.

Gish, John, and Nancy Stanley—Dec. 19, 1815.

Gish, John, and Polly Noftzinger, dau. David Noftzinger—March 27, 1816.

Gish, Samuel, and Sarah Smith—Feb. 26, 1817.

Givens, Elisha, and Hetty Peck, dau. Benjamin Peck—Dec. 26, 1802.

Givens, Isiah, and Elizabeth Webb—1797.

Givens, Joseph, and Ann Reynolds. John Reynolds, surety—Oct. 13, 1801.

Givens, William, and Polly Walker. Consent by an uncle, Henry Walker—June 2, 1799.

Glasglow, Robert, and CatherineT. Anderson, dau. William Anderson—March 27, 1820.

Glasburn, Glassburn, Glassbarn.

Glassburn, David, and Elizabeth Carpenter, dau. Zopher and Mary Carpenter—June 21, 1778.

Glassburn, John, and Mary Richardson. John Richardson, surety—Nov. 22, 1802.

Glenn, Patrick, and Jane FcCarroll, dau. James M'Carroll—April 18, 1797.

Goaden, Brooks, and Elizabeth Hickman, dau. Adam Hickman, of Rockbridge—Dec. 5, 1811.

Gofford, John, and Elizabeth Hughs—Jan. 16, 1781.

Gohsen, John, and Margaret Green. William Green, surety—Jan. 14, 1794.

Gohsen, James, and Agnes Cunninghom Harris, dau. Robert Harris, Jr—June 23, 1797.

Gohsen, James, and Jane McDavid. John McDavid, surety—1793.

Golden, Frederick, and Beddy Brown—Feb. 7, 1791.

Goldson, William, and Mary Cross—Dec. 9, 1784.

Goode, Jacob, and Elizabeth Houttz, dau. Leonard Houttz—Nov. 24, 1817.

Goode, John, and Barbara Werts, dau. John Werts—Feb. 10, 1821.

Goode, John, and Catherine Statler, dau. Abraham Statler—Aug. 29, 1806.

Goode, Thomas, and Hannah Saintentoffer. John Saintentoffer, surety—Nov. 24, 1817.

Goodman, Philip, and Mary Smith, widow of John Smith—Oct. 3, 1811.

Goodson, John, and Sarah Wickham. John Wickham (a brother), surety—Sept. 7, 1789.

Goodson, Thomas, and Elizabeth Poage. Robert Poage, surety—July 11, 1782.

Goodson, Thompson, and Mary Crawford, dau. James Crawford—Sept. 22, 1816.

Goodson, William, and Margaret Read, dau. Samuel Read—Jan. 12, 1790.

Goodson, William, and Elizabeth Wickham—July 13, 1784.

Goodwin, James, and Nancy McConnell—Dec. 17, 1799.

Goodwin, Joseph, and Mary Jenkins. John Jenkins, surety—March 27, 1820.

Goodwin, Peter, and Polly Mifford—Aug. 6, 1800.

Goodwin, Thomas, and Nelly Read, dau. Thomas Read—Jan. 16, 1804.

Goodwin, William, an Matty Read, dau. Thomas Read—Jan. 16, 1804.

Gordon, Daniel, and Polly Cartmill, dau. John Cartmill—Oct. 25, 1811.

Gordon, Giles, and Julia Ott, dau. George Ott, dec—Sept. 8, 1807.

Gordon, James, and Margaret Anderson—June 2, 1818.

Gordon, John, and Elinor Zirkle, dau. John Zirkle—Feb. 4, 1821.

Gordon, Richard, and Ann Ghant. Frederick Gaunt, surety—Jan. 4, 1801.

Gorman, Matthew, and Mary Little. Wh. Little, surety—Jan. 18, 1815.

Gorman, Patrick, and Frances Trotter—April 11, 1788.

Gowens, John, and Margaret Clarke, widow of Henry Clarke—Nov. 6, 1816.

Gowin, James, and Christina Vanover—Oct. 11, 1791.

Gowins, John, and Winey Bradford—May 26, 1819.

Grady, Burwell, and Patsy McNeal, dau. John McNeal—Sept. 7, 1809.

Grant, William, and Tillithy Gordon—Nov. 21, 1799. (Or Tillithy Jordon)

Graves (see Groves).

Graves, John, and Nancy C. McConnell—Aug. 19, 1820.

Graves, Richard, and Eliza Dennis. Edward Dennis, surety—Oct. 29, 1813.

Graves,, William, and Polly Goodman. James Goodman, surety—March 8, 1796.

Grawmer, Frederick, and Mary Green. Ed-

ward Green, surety—April 22, 1777.

Gray, George, and Betsy Tate, dau. John Tate—Aug. 26, 1817.

Gray, George, and Mary Davies. Joseph Davies, surety—Feb. 24, 1778.

Gray, Isaac, and Lucy Hardy, widow of George Hardy—Dec. 6, 1819.

Gray, James, and Eve Harvey, dau. Philip—March 14, 1814.

Gray, James, and Mary Harrison, dau. James Harrison—Jan. 31, 1811.

Gray, John, and Mary Harris, dau. Thomas Harris—Oct. 25, 1792.

Gray, John, and Sarah B. Moon, dau. John Moon—Dec. 14, 1814.

Gray, Joseph, and Elizabeth Coon, dau. Jacob Coon—Oct. 7, 1815.

Gray, William, and Mary Beaver—Oct. 3, 1796.

Graybill, John, and Polly Ovenchain, dau. Samuel Ovenchain—April 1, 1805.

Graybill, John, and Mary Huff, dau. Lewis Huff—Oct. 26, 1813.

Graybill, Solomon, and Caty Cline—April 19, 1800.

Greaver, William, and Polly Goodman—1796.

Green, Edward, and Elizabeth Woods, dau. Samuel Woods—Jan. 2, 1806.

Green, James, and Hannah Vandine, dau. Jacob Vandine, dec.—March 6, 1807.

Green, John, and Jemima Smith. Consent by Benj and Hannah Smith—May 3, 1795.

Green, Reuben, and Mary McConnell, dau. James McConnell—Oct. 13, 1807.

Green, William, and Peggy Cartmill, dau. John Cartmill—April 30, 1806.

Greenlee, Edward, and Hannah Greenlee. Alexander Greenlee, surety—July 15, 1792.

Greenlee, Francis, and Nancy Casteel. Abednigo C. Casteel, surety—Dec. 3, 1798.

Greenlee, James, and Jane McDavid, dau. John McDavid—April 1, 1793.

Greenlee, John, and Ruth Holstine, dau. Henry Holstine—Sept. 21, 1818.

Greenlee, John, and Ann Campbell—Sept. 29, 1780.

Greenwood, Henry B., and Elizabeth Prewit, dau. Obediah Prewit—Oct. 6, 1817.

Greenwood, William, and Phebe Combs, dau. Gilbert Combs—April 3, 1814.

Griffin, John C., and Mary Hancock, dau. Col. George Hancock—Dec. 23, 1805.

Griffith, John, and Bridget Gatey—May 30, 1801.

Griggs, John, and Mary Clancy. George Clancy, surety—March 7, 1783.

Grigsby, Joseph, and Mary A. W. Scott.

Fry—Oct. 8, 1805.

Groves (see Graves)

Groves, Joseph, and Phebe Combs, dau. Gilbert Combs—April 3, 1814.

Gualtney, Thomas, and Jane Sherrad, dau. Simon Sherral—Aug. 16, 1817.

Guin, Gwinn, Guin.

Guinn, Isiah, and Elizabeth Webb. John Webb, surety—May 15, 1797.

Guinn, William, and Polly Daugherty—Nov. 17, 1797.

Guinn, William, and Nancy Kimberling, dau. Palser Kimberling—June 11, 1798.

Gulliver, John, and Elizabeth Deardorf, dau. Peter Deardorf—March 18, 1805.

Guire, William, and Betsy Adams—Nov. 27, 1797.

Guire, William, and Polly Daugherty—1797. (See Guinn above.)

Gurtney, John, and Catherine Custer, dau. John Custer—June 9, 1806.

Guthrey, Alex. and Jane McFerran. Samuel McFerren, surety—Nov. 22, 1791. Father deceased—Dec. 8, 1812.

Grist, Joseph, and Sally Adney—May 8, 1818.

Grist, William, and Rebecca Hampton, dau. John Hampton—Mrach 30, 1819.

Gross, Adam. and Barbery Grove (orphan)—Feb. 13, 1798. (bound girl)

Cross, Adam. and Betsy Custer, dau. John Custer—Nov. 26, 1804.

Gross, Conrad, and Mary Bower, dau. Martin Bower, dec.—Dec. 12, 1814.

Gross, Isaac, and Elizabeth Lamb. Archabald Lamb. surety—May 3, 1794.

Gross, Jacob, and Mary Hypes. John Hypes, surety—Dec. 3, 1794.

Gross, John. and Elizabeth Grose, dau. Jacob Grose—Dec. 15, 1817.

Gross, John. and Polly Fields—March 6, 1822.

Ground, George, and Sarah Kinzle (19 yrs.), dau Chris. Kinzle—Nov. 10, 1798.

Ground, George, and Sally Fry, dau. Mathias

—H—

Hack Peter, and Sarah Flack. Peter Flack, surety—Aug. 13, 1798.

Hackett, Bazzel, and Jenny Williamson, dau. David Williamson, dec.—Feb. 28, 1803.

Hackett, John, and Elizabeth Biggs. John Biggs, surety—May 13, 1806.

Hackett, Thomas, and Eliabeth McCalister, dau. Peter McCalister—Feb. 18, 1803.

Haden (see Hayden)

Haden, Barthalomew, and Catherine Gholson, dau. Anthony Gholdson—June 16, 1801.

Hagins, John, and Sarah Coon, dau. Jacob

Coon, dec—June 21, 1816.

Hahn, Peter, and Hannah Peck, dau. Jacob Peck—Oct. 21, 1788.

Halderman, Christian, and Hetty Nave, dau. John Nave—Jan. 21, 1803.

Hall, Daniel, and Sarah Patterson—May 9, 1799.

Hall, John, and Jane Phillips, dau. Thomas Phillips—Aug. 12, 1822.

Hambeck, James, and Mary Crawford. Wm. Crawford, surety—Oct. 13, 1807.

Hamilton, Andrew, and Sarah C. Seldon—Nov. 8, 1800.

Hamilton, Gilbreath, and Elizabeth Law, widow of Jesse Law—July 29, 1807.

Hamilton, John, and Fanny Causalver (25 yrs)—Sept. 20, 1806.

Hamilton, John, and Elizazbeth Maxwell, widow of William—Aug. 24, 1818.

Hamilton, Joseph, and Sally Darnell (21 yrs) —March 11, 1806.

Hamilton, Samuel, and Nancy Robinson. John Robinson, surety—Aug. 21, 1800.

Hamilton, William, and Margaret Bell, dau. Victor Bell Sr.—July 21, 1796.

Hamilton, William, and Elizabeth Butcher—April 13, 1819.

Hammill, Robert, and Jean Ferguson, dau. Henry Ferguson of Bedford—Aug. 27, 1782.

Hammond, Peter, and Barbara Hypes—Dec. 8, 1789.

Hammond, Peter, and Margaret Housman, dau. Christian Housman—March 20, 1822.

Hammill, Robert, and Jean Ferguson, dau. Henry Ferguson, of Bedford—Aug. 27, 1782.

Hampton, John, Jr. and Lydia Miller, dau. Peter Miller—June 22, 1813.

Hance. Henry, and Catherine Coffman, dau. Henry Coffmna—July 26, 1803.

Hancock. George, and Margaret Strother. Consent by mother, Mary Lockland—Aug. 24, 1781.

Handley, Alexander. and Anna Reynolds, widow— Feb. 27, 1802.

Handley. Samuel, and Betsy Frantz—April 15, 1797.

Hanes, Haines - see Haines etc.

Hanes, Henry, and Sarah Potts (over 21). Jacob Hanes, surety—Jan 12, 1798.

Hanes, Isaac, and Nancy Sisler, dau. Thomas Sisler—March 12, 1805.

Haines, Isaac, and Elizabeth Floyd, dau. Morris Floyd—Nov. 10, 1818.

Hanes, Jacob, and Catherine Peightal, dau. Frederick Peightal—Jan. 18, 1790.

Hanks, John C. and Mary Dicks, widow—April 14, 1818.

Hank, John, and Rebecca Price, dau. Thomas Price—March 3, 1817.

Hanna-Hannah.

Hanna, John, and Elizazbeth Townsley, dau. Thomas, dec. and Elizabeth Tosh—July 28, 1818.

Hannah, Joseph, and Harriet Allen, dau. John Allen—Nov. 30, 1812.

Hannah. Patterson, and Elizabeth Evans, dau. Peter Evans—March 7, 1804.

Hannon, Esom, and Mary Brown, dau. Thomas Brown—Dec. 26, 1815.

Hannon, Esom, and Mary Greenlee, dau. William Greenlee—Sept. 11, 1783.

Hannon, John, and Keziah Brown, dau. Thomas Brown—March 3, 1817.

Hannon, Thomas, and Elizabeth Henry. John Henry, surety—Dec. 28, 1781.

Hannon, Thomas, and Elizabeth Gharst, dau. Jacob Gharst—Feb. 2, 1818.

Hannon, William, and Susannna Griste (or Grisle), dau. Samuel—March 8, 1814.

Hannon, Sephyr, and Mary Shawver. Adam Shawver, surety—May 12, 1798.

Hansbarger, Bostin, and Elizabeth Pitzer, dau. Abraham—Sept. 30, 1818.

Hansbarger, Jacob, and Experience Poage, dau. George Poage—Oct. 12, 1811.

Hansbarger, John, and Elizabeth Nicewonder, dau. John Nicewonder—Jan. 30, 1804.

Hanson, John, and Mary Wall, dau. Conrad Wall—April, 1783.

Hanson, Samuel, and Elizabeth Pierce, dau. Edward Pierce—June 23, 1804.

Hanson, William, and Anne Craig, dau. George Craig—Dec. 3, 1796.

Harbison, James, and Ann Looney, dau. Absolum Looney—Oct. 15, 1785.

Hardbarger, Henry, and Polly Brook, dau. Philip Brook—Jan. 11, 1811.

Harden, George, and Lucy Galloway, dau. Benjamin Galloway—Aug. 15, 1803.

Hardy, Jonathan, and Rebecca Stoner, dau. Daniel Stoner—Jan. 28, 1811.

Hardy, Thomas, and Elizabeth Crawford—May 30, 1799.

Harger, George, and Phebe Grist, dau. John Grist—June 14, 1814.

Harkins, George, and Narcissa Merrett, dau. Samuel Merrett—Nov. 26, 1817.

Harmon, Andrew, and Sarah Waits, dau. George Waits, dec.—Dec. 19, 1815.

Harmon, Henry, and Mary Burke. Andrew Burke, surety— Nov. 20, 7195.

Harmon, Jacob, nad Elizabeth Heckle—Nov. 13, 1793.

Harmon, Peter, and Mary Biggs, dau. Ed-

ward Biggs—Dec. 29, 1802.

Harper, Ebenezer, and Margaret Cregg. Alex Cregg, surety—Feb. 24, 1798.

Harper, Joseph, and Mary Mason, widow of Martin Mason—Dec. 31, 1799.

Harris, Cephas, and Betty Richardson—Sept. 22, 1805.

Harris, Emmanuel, and Catherine Evans, dau. Peter Evans, dec.—Aug. 22, 1815.

Harris, Jesse, and Betsy Richardson—Sept. 22, 1805.

Harris, John, and Nary Leatherdale. John Leatherdale, surety—Oct. 25, 1779.

Harris Samuel, and Elizabeth Tosh, widow of Jonathan Tosh—Jan. 19, 1819.

Harrison, Cary, and Elizabeth Fleming, dau. Col. Wm. Fleming—Nov. 4, 1793.

Hrrison, John, and Nancy Hanson, dau. William Hanson—Jan. 11, 1810.

Harrison, Reuben, and Mary Hickenbottom. Moses Hickenbottom, surety—July 3, 1789.

Harrison, Thomas, and Margaret Billups—Jan. 18. 1788.

Harrison, Thomas, and Hannah Dennis—March 7, 1779.

Harsh, Jacob, and Jean Weathers—Feb. 19, —1787.

Harsh, Nathan, and Hannah Walker, widow —Nov. 19, 1807.

Harshbarger, Christian, and Susanna Garman, widow of John Garman—Dec. 26, 1804.

Harshbarger, Henry and Barbara Kilmere, dau. George Kilmere—Nov. 9, 1813.

Harshbarger, Jacob, and Sarah Amen, dau. Michael Amen—Oct. 22, 1814.

Harshbarger, Jacob, and Elizabeth Sullenbarger, widow of David—Feb. 15, 1818.

Harshbarger, Jacob, and Elizabeth Beckner, dau. Jonathan Beckner—Oct. 12, 1809.

Harshbarger, Samuel, and Polly Kinzey, dau. Jacob Kinzey—Sept. 24, 1811.

Harshbarger, William, and Sally Blount, dau. Nathaniel Blount—Sept. 28, 1818.

Harter, John, and Rachel Gaunt. Henry Harter, surety—May 25, 1801.
See Heartman

Hartman, Abraham, and Polly Kittinger, dau. Rudolph Kittinger—Nov. 25, 1819.

Hartman, George, and Elizabeth Biggs—May 23, 1796.

Hartman, Jacob, and Elizabeth Shewry, dau. John Shewry—Nov. 27, 1820.

Hartman, John, and Polly Carroll, dau. William Carroll, March 7, 1812.

Hartman, John, and Catherine Gharst, dau. Jacob Gharst—May 14, 1812.

Hartman, John, and Elizabeth Little, John,

son of Frederick. Elizabeth, dau. William—Aug. 17, 1798.

Hartman, Nicholas, and Mary Russel, dau. James Russel—May 16, 1812.

Harvey, James, and Elizabeth Carper, dau. Nicholas Carper—July 21, 1790.

Harvey, Lewis, and Frances T. Burwell, dau. Nathaniel Burwell—Sept. 25, 1807.

Harvey, Matthew, and Magdalene Hawkins, dau. Martha Harvey—Aug. 18, 1788.

Harvey, Robert, and Martha Hawkins, widow —Dec. 9, 1788.

Hasten, James, and Betsy Harris—Dec. 11, 1801.

Hatton, Samuel, and Elizabeth Armstrong, widow of Thomas—Feb. 6, 1807.

Hauspeck (Hausseck?) Peter, and Catherine Read—Sept. 9, 1793.

Hawkins, John, and Sarah Lauderdale, dau. James Lauderdale—Oct. 13, 1793.

Haydon, Stephen, and Lydia Compton—Oct. 15, 1785.

Haymaker, Philip, and Elizabeth Fizer. Henry Fizer, surety—Feb. 12, 1798.

Hayne, Christopher, and Alice Vanmetre—Aug. 28, 1784.

Haynes, Austin, and Eliabeth Minnick, dau. Benjamin Minnick—Feb. 15, 1814.

Haynes, John, and Catherine Clack—June 2, 1788.

Haynes, William, and Caty Shanklin, dau. Richard Shanklin—Jan. 22, 1790.

Hays, James, and Rebecca Bilbro, dau. William Bilbro—Feb. 22, 1806.

Hays, William, and Sarah Coon, dau. Jacob Coon, dec. June 21, 1816.

Hayslip, John, and Peggy Lockhart, dau. William Lockhart—March 21, 1806.

Hayslip, John, and Peggy Lyons, dau. William Lyons—Nov. 8, 1809.

Head, John, and Nancy Old, dau. Edward Old—Feb. 8, 1809.

Heartman, Jacob, and Margaret Beard. Martin Beard, surety—Nov. 12, 1793.

Heck, Daniel, and Nancy Calhoon, dau. Charles Calhoon—Oct. 11, 1812.

Heck, David, and Metelda Spitler, dau. Jacob Spitler—March 25, 1811.

Heck, Frederick, and Nancy Fry, dau. Mathas Fry—June 25, 1813.

Heck, Peter, and Mary Hoofnauger, widow of Jacob—Dec. 4, 1811.

Heck, Peter, Jr., and Anne Frantz, dau. Daniel Frantz—June 5, 1815.

Hedrick, Charles, and Mary Vanmetre. Isaac Vanmetre, surety—Oct. 5, 1798.

Heistand, Jacob, and Eve Landis, dau. Peter

Landis—Oct. 16, 1811.

Helams, Leonard, and Elizabeth Page. Father dec.—Dec. 22, 1791.

Helms, John, and Sarah Woods, dau. Samuel Woods—March 25, 1818.

Helmantaller, Peter, and Margaret Brenner. Jacob Helmantaller, surety—Nov. 25, 1793.

Henderson, Andrew, and Sarah Adkins, dau. Molly Adkins—June 9, 1794.

Henderson, Alexander, and Elizabeth Humphries. Uriah Humphries, surety—Feb. 23, 1795.

Henderson, John, and Martha Kimberling—Dec. 30, 1797.

Henderson, Robert, and Harriot Lackland, dau. Elisha Lackland—June 28, 1806.

Henderson, William ,and Isabella Crawford, dau. Josiah Crawford—Feb. 19, 1817.

Henderson, Zacheriah, and Susanna Magott, dau. John Magott—May 4, 1805.

Henry, James, and Nancy Blunt, dau. Nathaniel Blunt—Nov. 24, 1817.

Henry, John, and Elizabeth Mitchell, dau. William Mitchell—July 16, 1805.

Henry, John, and Hannah Custer, dau. Abram Custer. James Henry, surety—Dec. 25, 1790.

Henry, John, and Rosanna Jarrott—Oct. 2, 1787.

Henry, Sabre, and Eleanor Flora—March 9, 1801.

Henry Samuel, and Elizabeth Salmon. Jacob Salmon—Dec. 18, 1790.

Henry, William, and Bathsheba Owens—June 8, 1802.

Henry, William, and Elizabeth Jones—June 14, 1780.

Henson, John, and Mary Wall, dau. Conrad Wall—April 10, 1783.

Henson, Samuel, and Anne Wolf, dau. Michael Wolf—May 14, 1803.

Henson, William, and Savilly Duckwyle—March 1, 1785.

Hess, Michael, and Hannah Frederick—Dec. 31, 1797.

Hessler, Henry (son of George), and Betsy Kessler, dau. John Kessler—Dce. 9, 1809.

Hewitt, John, and Margaret Hewitt, dau. Pat Hewitt—Nov. 19, 1794.

Hewitt, Reese, and Polly Fore, dau. Phillip Fore, dec.—July 25, 1810.

Hickle, George, and Agnes Lemmon, dau. Frederick Lemmon—Oct. 6, 1818.

Hickle, Jacob, an Susanna Lybert, dau. John Lybert—Sept. 4, 1810.

Hickle, John, and Catherine Specard, dau. Michael Specard—April 9, 1806.

Hickok, Morris, and Sally Fleager, dau. Michael Fleager—July 1, 1822.

Hicks, Jacob, and Barbara Harshbarger, widow of Henry—Mrahc 14, 1816.

Hicks,, John, and Peggy Simpson—Jan. 17, 1800.

Higgins, Peter, and Polly Beale, dau. Tavanor Beale—1802.

Higinbottom, William, and Katherine Stuart Bellew. Meredith Bellew, surety—Ja.n 17, 1791.

Hill, Cholin, and Julia McCrosky, dau. George McCrosky—March 51, 1814.

Hill, James, and June Culbertson—July 8, 1772.

Hill, Spencer, and Mary Rutherford, dau. Thomas Rutherford, dec—Jan. 24, 1788.

Hill, Thomas, and Elizabeth Dunason, widow —April 10, 1800.

Hill, William, and Rachel Poage—March 20, 1789.

Hillam, Daniel, and Lucy Gaunt—June 28, 1797.

Hilles, John, and Eunicey Ritchey, dau. William Ritchey—Sept. 16, 1793.

Himelock, Peter, and Nancy Eller, dau. Jacob Eller—Feb. 23, 1820.

Hindlighter, John, and Madlina Deal. George Deal, surety—March 8, 1796.

Hiner, Abraham, and Christina Boblett, dau. dau. Michael Boblett—May 27, 1801.

Hines, Daniel, and Polly Wrightman, dau. John Wrightman, dec.—Oct. 27, 1817.

Hinkle, Lot, and Rosanna Gharst, dau. Jacob Gharst—May 29, 1821.

Hinton, William, and Catherine Kerns, dau. Jacob Kerns—July 20, 1807.

Hite, William, and Elizabeth Brown, dau. John Brown—Feb. 14, 1804.

Hively, James, and Frances Huffman, dau. John Huffman—Aug. 22, 1818.

Hively, John, and Sally Lake, dau. Eziral Lake, dec.—Jan. 11, 1820.

Hodd, Thomas, and Katherine Kelly—April 17, 1779.

Hoffman, Jacob, and Ann Mmen, dau. Daut Amen—March 30, 1801.

Holderman, Abraham, and Sally Neff, dau. John Neff—Sept. 19, 1807.

Holderman, John, and Mary Harris, dau. Robert, Jr.—Jan. 23, 1797.

Holloway, Haynes, and Mary Hinton, dau. James Hinton, of Ky.—Oct. 12, 1813.

Holstine, David, and D........ Walker. Arch Walker, surety—Dec. 9, 1822.

Holstine, George, and Ann Smith, dau. Jacob Smith—Jan. 3, 1822.

Holstine, Henry, and Margaret Frame. Consent by Henry Holstine and David Frame ("to our children being joined together")— July 2, 1781.

Holstine, John, and Patsy Staut. Henry Holstine, surety—Sept. 27, 1801.

Holstine, Peter, and Elizabeth McClure, dau. Richard McClure—Dec. 16, 1817.

Holstine, Stephen, and Jane Looney—June 1, 1781.

Holstine, Stephen, and Elizabeth Price, dau. Thomas Price—Dec. 2, 1818.

Hoole, David, and Ann Howell. David Howell, surety—Dec. 31, 1799.

Hoosey, John, and Magdalene Koal—Nov. 28, 1801.

Hoover, Mathias, and Ann Switzer. William Switzer, surety—Nov. 21, 1801.

Hopakin, Jacob, and Magdalene Shatzer, dau. Philip Hhatzer—July 30, 1805.

Hopkins, Moses, and Elizabeth Brown, dau. William Brown—April 3, 1816.

Horn, John, and Nancy Sheets, dau. Jacob Sheets—April 16, 1814.

Houberson, David, and Catherine Dougherty, dau. Rebeckah Dougherty—June 25, 1773.

Hough, Stephen, and Elizabeth Phillips. John Philips, surety—Feb. 25, 1803.

Houson, Samuel, and Elizabeth Pierce, dau. Edward Pierce, dec.—July 23, 1804.

Houts, Leonard, and Elizabeth Frantz, dau. Henry Frantz—Sept. 19, 1805.

Houtz, John, and Elizabeth Noftzinger, dau. David Noftzinger—Sept. 24, 1821.

Howard, Elisha, and Mile Gile—Jan. 13, 1818.

Howard, Ezekiel, and Mary Ann Goodman— Feb. 5, 1785.

Howard, James, and Sally Myers, dau. Jacob Myers—Feb. 5, 1811.

Howard, John, and Rebecca Anderson, dau. Robert Anderson—April 25, 1791.

Howard, John, and Sarah Fruster. Consent by mother, Margurett—Feb. 28, 1797.

Howard, John, and Barbara Surber, dau. Rosanna Surber—Nov. 16, 1789.

Howard, Matthew, and Barbara Baughman, dau. Henry Baughman—March 30, 1802.

Howard, Thomas, and Pattey or Patty Hughes, dau. William Hughes—May 28, 1793.

Howbert, Michael, and Hannah Peffley, dau. Jacob Peffley—Aug. 31, 1818.

Howell, David, and Jane Allen, dau. Daniel and Jane Allen—Nov. 3, 1804.

Howell, Jesse, and Anna Horn, dau. Charles Horn—Nov. 3, 1804.

Howell, Samuel, and Elizabeth Newell— March 14, 1816.

Howery, Daniel, and Susanna Way (Wax?),
dau. Peter—Nov. 25, 1801.

Howery, Daniel, and Mary Feller, April 19,
1810.

Howry, Jacob, and Catherine Feller, widow—
Nov. 1, 1803.

Howry, Jacob, and Martha Gaunt, dau. John
Gaunt—Jan. 15, 1803.

Howry, Jacob, and Polly Huff—Aug. 16, 1816.

Howery, Jacob, and Susannah Clair—April
21, 1798.

Howry, Michael, and Christeen Hartman—
Aug. 14, 1786.

Howery, Samuel, and Mary Sifford—Aug. 17,
1792.

Hudson, Jesse, and Jane Taylor, dau. Isaac
and Jane Taylor—Dec. 7, 1819.

Hudson, Jesse, and Martha Wilson, dau. William Wilson—Nov. 1, 1808.

Hudson, Thomas, and Nancy Johnston, dau.
William Johnston, dec.—Jan. 28, 1805.

Hudson, Timothy, and Cathran Winelf-Minelf—1794.

Huff, Abraham, and Hannah Kinzey, dau.
Daniel Kinzey—May 18, 1819.

Huff, David, and Mary Kinzey, dau. David
Kinzey—Oct. 11, 1813.

Huff, Samuel, and Nancy Noftzinzer, dau.
Peter Noftzinger—Oct. 28,1816.

Huffman, John, and Nancy Cooper, dau.
Charles Cooper—Aug. 24, 1818.

Huffman, John, and Priscy Gray, dau. James
Gray—Nov. 23, 1807.

Huffman, Thomas, and Margaret Lemmon,
dau. Frederick Lemmon—Nov. 4, 1820.

Hughes, George, and Margaret Johnston,
dau. David Johnston—Nov. 9, 1790.

Hughes, James, and Mary Simpson, dau.
James and Jean Simpson—May 3, 1781.

Hughes, Randol, and Elizabeth Henry—Aug.
20, 1791.

Hulse, James, and Peggy Henry—March 5,
1781.

Humphreys, Henry, and Elizabeth Howard,
dau. John Howard—March 10, 1812.

Humphreys, William, and Ruthe Persinger,
dau. Henry Persinger—Nov. 26, 1821.

Hunter, James D. and Hannah Kilmer, dau.
George Kilmer, Sr.—Jan. 19, 1822.

Huntsman, Richard, and Nancy Duncan,
dau. Robert Duncan, dec.—Dec. 21, 1808.

Hurley, Timothy (see Hudson above).

Hutchinson, Bennett, and Elizabeth Hannon,
dau. Esom Hannon—Nov. 24, 1814.

Hutcheson, James and Elizabeth Francisco—
March 27, 1784.

Hutcheson, Robert, and Elinor Eakin, dau.

Redmon Eakin—Jan. 23, 1807.

Hutson, Elijah, and Jane King, dau. William
King—Jan. 19, 1822.

Hyner, John, and Catherine Weaver, dau.
Leonard and Polly Weaver—Feb. 9, 1796.

Hypes, Henry, and Patience Reynolds. John
Reynolds, surety—Feb. 28, 1795.

Hypes, John, and Elizabeth Wimond (21 yrs)
—Aug. 13, 1796.

Hypes, Nicholas, and Rebeccah Dilman, dau.
Daniel Dilman—May 29, 1815.

Hypes, Peter, and Sarah Dodd, dau. William
Dodd—April 8, 1816.

—I—

Icenberry, John, and Susan Frantz, dau.
Henry Frantz—June 18, 1821.

Icynhower, Jacob, and Esther Lantz, dau.
Peter Lantz—Feb. 3, 1810.

Idle, Henry, and Elizabeth Robinson, dau.
John Robinson—Jan. 15, 1806.

Ingle, Henry, and Sarah Hanson. David
Hanson, surety—May 8, 1793.

Ingle, Mathias, and Barbara Weaver—May
30, 1797.

Inglehart, George, and Betsy Powers, dau.
Yancy—July 22. 1813.

Ireland, William, and Sally Coon, dau.
Michael Coon—June 11, 1805.

Isenhower, Michael, and Isabelle Mitchell,
dau. Alexander Mitchell, dec.—Feb. 18, 1804.

Issom, Abner, and Susanna Hardy, dau.
Thomas Hardy—Nov. 27, 1810.

Isenbarger, Henry, and Mary Markey, dau.
Nicholas Markey—March 30, 1814.

—J—

Jackson, Samuel, and Margaret Stover, dau.
William Stover—March 1, 1806.

Jackson, Thomas, and Elizabeth Faught,
dau. Casper Faught—Aug. 31, 1786.

James, Daniel, and Elizabeth Bandy. Richard
Bandy, surety—Oct. 13, 1801.

James, Elisha Christian, and Rebecca Wolfingbarger, dau. Peter Wolfingbarger—Jan.
3, 1805.

(Bond give name Christian. Bond says
Elisha.)

James, Jonathan, and Polly Bandy, dau. John
Bandy—April 23, 1810.

James, Joseph, and Elizabeth Hemming,
widow—Sept. 5, 1815.

James, Thomas, and Barbara Britz, dau.
Adam Britz—Nov. 4, 1806.

Jamison, John, and Elizabeth Douglas, dau.
John Douglas—Feb. 24, 1807.

Jamison, Robert, and Agnes Edgar. John Edgar, surety—March 22, 1791.

Jarrett, Abraham, and Elizabeth Hughes. Consent by Thomas Hughes—May 5, 1791.

Jarrett, David, and Jane Graham, dau. James and Flouno Graham—June 6, 1792.

Jarrett, Robert, and Martha Kyle, dau. Joseph Kyle—Sept. 30, 1802.

Jarris, Franklin, and Elizabeth Scott, dau. Tom Scott—Aug. 1, 1789.

Jasper, Isaac, and Susannah Sovaine, dau. Abraham Sovaine—May 20, 1797.

Jenkins, John, and Rachel Henry (or Howry). Samuel McElaney, surety—July 29, 1816.

Jeter, Henry, and Anne Craft, dau. John Craft, dec.—Dec. 3, 1805.

Jeter, Ira, and Sarah White, dau. Samuel White—July 23, 1820.

Jewell, Thomas, and Elizabeth Grimes (over 21)—May 18, 1796.
(Tradition says "Elizabeth Graham")

Jewell, Thomas, and Nancy Lewis. Joseph Lewis, surety—Sept. 8, 1800.

Johnson, Castleton, and Nancy Eubank, dau. John—Dev. 21, 1819.

Johnson, Charles C. (of Washington Co), and Elizabeth M. Preston, dau. John Preston—Dec. 30, 1822.

Johnson, James, and Magdalena Kilmer, dau. George Kilmer—January 9, 1810.

Johnson, James, and Betty Sell, dau. Thomas Sell—Oct. 18, 1810.

Johnson, John, and Elinor Wilson—Sept. 2, 1776.

Johnson, John, and Catrin Dewitt—Nov. 31, 1787.

Johnson, Sylvanius, and Peggy Madison, dau. Thomas Madison, dec.—Nov. 30, 1805.

Johnson, Thomas, and Rebecca Oldham. Father dec.—June 26, 1810.

Johnson, Zacheriah, and Elizabeth Rowland, dau. James Rowland—Dec. 16, 1810.

Johnston, James, and Milly Pate, dau. Jeremiah Pate, dec.—Dec. 10, 1811.

Johnston, John, and Elizabeth Wysonburg, dau. Christopher, dec.—Aug. 3, 1819.

Johnston, Orsmus, and Anna Henry, dau. William Henry—Sept. 30, 1805.

Johnston, William, and Sarah Haynes. Joseph Haynes, surety—April 7, 1800.

Johnston, William, and Susanna Harrison—April 27, 1797.

Johnston, William, and Sarah McCoy, dau. Thomas—June 2, 1813.

Jones, Allen, and Jean Caldwell, dau. Mary Caldwell—Oct. 10, 1792.

Jones, Allen, and Susanna Peck, dau. John

Peck—July 29, 1809.

Jones, Ambrose, Jr., and Margaret Mifford—Oct. 3, 1800.

Jones, Edward, and Susanna Painter,, dau. John Painter—Dec. 17, 1819.

Jones, Francis, and Mary Glover, dau. Agnes Glover, of Spottsylvania Co., Va.—Aug. 15, 1805.

Jones, Henry, and Mary Rutherford—March 23, 1797.

Jones, James, and Polly Brickey, dau. Peter Brickey—April 7, 1807.

Jones, Joseph, and Susanna Wright—April 14, 1794.

Jones, Richard, and Jane Buckanan—July 1, 1782.

Jones, Recard, and Barbara Snider, dau. Jacob Snider—Jan. 6, 1813.

Jones, Samuel, and Catherine Fostor (or Foslor)—July 11, 1791.

Jones, Shedrick, and Susanna Alverman, dau. James Alverman—Sept. 3, 1794.

Jones, William, and Jane Reynolds, dau. James Reynolds, dec.—Nov. 30, 1821.

Jordon, Samuel, and Eliza Scott, dau. James Scott, dec.—Sept. 27, 1811.

Jordon, Thomas, and Lydia McNeel. Hugh McNeel, surety—Oct. 10, 1783.

Jordon, William, and Mary Gish—May 20, 1820.

—K—

Karnes, Jacob, and Ann Coin. John Karnes and John Coin, sureties—Oct. 4, 1797.

Karnes, Moses, and Aggy Thompson, dau. Joseph Thompson—Aug. 11, 1812.

Kayton, John, and Rebeckah Moore, dau. William Moore—June 30, 1821.

Keasea, Arch, and Susanna Nox, dau. Elisha Nox—Aug. 31, 1789.

Keefauver, David, and Mary Ray, dau. Evan Ray—Sept. 1, 1818.

Keefauver, Peter, and Susanna Nidy, dau. George Nidy—Jan. 14, 1820.

Kaffer, Jacob, and Margaret Fizer—June 14, 1792.

Kelly-Kelley.

Kelly, Andrew, and Sarah Wall. John Wall, surety—Feb. 9, 1796.

Kelly, Henry, and Patsy Combs—Jan. 29, 1819.

Kelly, Isaac, and Rebecca Woods, dau. Robert Woods, surety—Nov. 15, 1775.

Kelly, James, and Betsy Garman, dau. John Garman—Dec. 27, 1809.

Kelly, John, and Elizabeth Coon, dau. Michael—June 15, 1813.

Kelley, John, and Lucy Pierce. William Dodd,

surety—Oct. 7, 1795.

Kelly, John, and Lucinda Colter, dau. Samuel Colter—Nov. 4, 1819.

Kelly, Joseph, and Dinah Woods, dau Joseph Woods—June 2, 1788.

Kelly, Thomas, and Betsy Bishop, dau. Jacob Bishop—Sept. 25, 1809.

Kemm - See Kimm.

Kemm, George, and Polly Helms, dau. Daniel Helms —July 23, 1810. (See Kimm.)

Kennaday, Benjamin, and Mary Fisher, dau. John Fisher—Jan. 11, 1802.

Kannaday, John, and Marth McNeel. James McNeel, surety—April 27, 1772.

Kenner, Lawrence S., and Lucy A. Winston, dau. William Winston, dec.—Oct. 15, 1810.

Kent, John, and Rachel Barnett. James Barnett, surety—Dec. 21, 1782.

Kepler (see Kessler).

Kepler, Abraham, and Susanna Wiseman, dau. Frederick Wiseman—Sept. 21, 1816.

Kepler, George and Rachel Lamb, dau. Archabald Lamb—Oct. 9, 1806.

Kerr, John, and Jane Sharg (lawful age)— Jan. 29, 1771.

Kerr, Samuel, and Isabella Ledgerwood, dau. John Ledgerwood—Dec. 16, 1779.

Kesler, Kessler, etc. See Kepler.)

Kesler, Abraham, and Caty Hester. George Hester, surety—Oct. 20, 1800.

Kesler, Benjamin, and Margaret Clear. Consent by Susanna Clear—Nov. 19, 1795.

Kesler, Christian, and Mary Clear. Consent by Susanna Clear—Oct. 21, 1793.

Kesler, Daniel, and Rebecca Rightman— March 7, 1793.

Kesler, Daniel, and Catherine Black, dau. Jacob Black—Aug. 5, 1817.

Kesler, David, and Sarah Cox, dau. Allen Cox—April 9, 1792.

Kessler, Jacob, and Catherine Brough, dau. Daniel Brough—April 29, 1816.

Kessler, Jacob, and Barbara Bower, dau. Philip Bower—Oct. 4, 1819.

Kesler, Jacob, and Catherine Brown, dau. Christopher Brown—Feb. 27, 1813.

Kessler, John, and Nancy McCray—Jan. 9, 1800.

Kessler, John, and Elizabeth Housman, dau. Christian—Aug. 7, 1813.

Kessler, Joseph, and Mary Magdalene Spessard, dau. Henry Spessard—Sept. 23, 1820.

Kessler, Peter, and Elizabeth Cifford, dau. Peter Cifford—Feb. 1, 1804.

Keys, Joseph, and Elizabeth Fleager, dau. Michael Fleager—April 7, 1814.

Keys, Joseph, and Mary Gurtner, dau. Philip

Gurtner, dec.—Dec. 23, 1817.

Keyser, James, and Lucinda Gillespie, dau. Robert Gillespie—Jan. 17, 1821.

Kilmere, George, and Caty Mould, dau. George Mould, dec.—March 30, 1811.

Kilmore, George, and Elizabeth Harshbarger, dau. Christian Harshbarger—Sept. 3, 1816.

Kimberling, Adam, and Mary Reed, dau. William and Ruthe Reed—Feb. 20, 1804.

Kimberling, Jacob, and Harriet Richey, dau. Robert Richey—Jan 2, 1822.

Kimberling, James, and Nancy Humphries, dau. Uriah Humphries. Palsar Kimberling, surety—Feb. 24, 1798.

Kimberling, John, and Jenny Clapsaddle, dau. George Clapsaddle—March 7, 1810.

Kimberling, Paulson, and Sarah Wright, dau. Peter Wright—Jan. 6, 1777.

Kimmerly, Samuel, and Mary Ryford—Oct. 21, 1784.

Kimes, Felty, and Elizabeth Custen. Abraham Custen, surety—Nov. 10, 1798.

Kimm see Kemm).

Kimm, George, and Sarah Fields ("over 21") —Aug. 19, 1803.

Kimm, Thomas, and Mary Centz, dau. Jacob Centz—Jan. 4, 1814.

Kincaid, James, and Elizabeth Edwards, dau. John Edwards. Wm. Kincaid, surety—Oct. 30, 1790.

Kincaid, John, and Aley Elliott. John Elliott, surety—July 26, 1787.

Kincaid, Robert (son of Robert), and Backy Wright, dau. Peter Wright—June 13, 1786.

Kincaid (see Kinkhead).

King, Charles, and Rebecca Bear—Aug. 21, 1784.

King, James Jno, and Sarah Goodson—Oct. 12, 1782.

King, John, and Isabel Parsinger, dau. Chris. Parsinger, dec.—Nov. 3, 1808.

Kingar (Wingar), James, and Margarett Butt, dau. Anthony Butt—Aug. 23, 1821.

Kinkhead, Andrew, and Mary Caldwell, dau. Samuel Caldwell—May 9, 1777.

Kinny, David, and Nancy Harshbarger, dau. Christian Harshbarger—April 4, 1818.

Kinsey, Abraham, and Catherine Esmonde. Samuel Kinsey, surety—June 14, 1798.

Kinsie, John, and Sally Myers, dau. John Myers—Sept. 4, 1821.

Kinzer, David, and Margaret Etzrath—Aug. 9, 1799.

Kepley, James, and Anna West, dau. Benjamin West—Aug 3, 1787.

Kerfman, John, and Polly Painter, dau.

Henry Painter—June 7, 1813.

Kirk, John, and Elizabeth O'Brian—Dec. 31, 1787.

Kirkpatrick, Andrew, and Jean Crawford. Wm. Crawford, surety—Sept. 18, 1798.

Kirkpatrick, Thomas, and Margaret Weir, dau. James Weir—Jan. 29, 1807.

Kitchen, Alexander, and Agnes Haynes, dau. Joseph Haynes—Feb. 31, 1807.

Kittenger, David, and Peggy Helms, dau. John Helms—Nov. 8, 1819.

Kittinger, Jacob, and Sally Forest, dau. James Forest—Jan. 2, 1806.

Kittinger, John, and Catherine Shaver, dau. Andrew Shaver, dec.—Sept. 2, 1822.

Kittinger, Martin (son of Rudolph), and Catherine Yeast—March 14, 1797.

Kittinger, Rudolph, and Mary Darby, widow of James Darby—Dec. 4, 1815.

Kittinger, Sampel, and Elizabeth Hartman, dau. John Hartman—Feb. 1, 1816

Kittinger, William, and Mary Ferguson. Consent by Mary Ferguson—Jan. 31, 1807.

Kizer, Henry, and Sarah Linkenhoger—Dec. 7, 1799.

Kizer (Kiser), Isaac, and Catherine Coon, dau. Jacob Coon—Aug. 29, 1812.

Knode, George, and Barbara Dolmon, dau. Henry Dolmon—May 12, 1817.

Knode, Michael, and Mary Young, dau. Nicholas Young—April 17, 1817.

Know, James, an Hannah McKutchen—1809.

Knox, Elisha, and Ruth Reed, widow Wm. Reed—April 27, 1807.

Knox, John, and Martha Hanson. Samuel Hanson, surety—Dec. 2, 1800.

Knox, Reuben, and Elizabeth Edgars, dau. Sarah Edgars—Dec. 6, 1813.

Knox, Thomas, and Milly McFadden—Dec. 7, 1787.

Kurfman, Peter, and Ranne Rouck, dau. George Rouck—Oct. 8, 1810.

Kyle, Barclay, and Jane McDonald, dau. Edward—April 22, 1813.

Kyle, Christopher, and Hetty McFerran, Aug. 7, 1820.

Kyle, David, and Betsy Kyle, dau. Joseph Kyle—April 26, 1791.

Kyle, Dinguid, and Margaret Pitzer, dau. John Pitzer—Feb. 3, 1808.

Kyle, James, and Harriet McDonald, dau. Edw. McDonald—Aug. 8, 1816.

Kyle, Jeremiah, and Mary Kyle. Wm. Kyle, surety—March 18, 1793.

Kyle, John, and Polly Green, dau. Edward Green—May 13, 1786.

Kyle, Robert, and Sarah Reynolds, dau. John

Reynolds—June 15, 1788.

Kyle, Robert, and Mary T. Harvey, dau. Matthew Harvey—Dec. 9, 1818.

—L—

Lacey, William, and Hannah Evans—Jan. 12, 1787.

Lackey, Nathan, and Mary Lackey, dau. James Lackey—1803.

Lackey, Thomas, and Susanna Henry, dau. John Henry—Dec. 21, 1777.

La force, Moncier, and Catherine Sutherland, dau. James Sutherland—Dec. 12, 1802.

La force, Rene, Jr. (son Rene La force, Sr.), and Anne Robinson (min ret. Agnes)—March 10, 1774.

La force, William, and Sarah Goodwin. Consent by Mary Goodwin—July 11, 1791.

Lake, John, and Jane Smith—Feb. 14, 1779.

Lake, Timothy, and Polly Coffman, dau. Henry Coffman—Dec. 12, 1814.

Lamb, Richard, and Esther Amyx, dau. Samuel Amyx—Nov. 13, 1813.

Lambert, George, and Eve Firestone, dau. Eve Firestone—Dec. 4, 1809.

Landis, Peter, and Sally Kelly, dau George Kelly, dec.—March 3, 1807.

Landridge, Abraham, and Jane Kelly, dau. George Kelly—Jan. 4, 1819.

Lane, Janes, and Martha Jack, dau. William Jack—May 26, 1778.

Lane, James, and Nancy Woodruff—Jan. 10, 1815.

Lane, Jessee, and Elizabeth Cloyd, dau. Michael Cloyd—Jan. 19, 1804.

Lanius, Adam, and Polly Dunbar. Consent by Mary Dauson of Monroe Co.—May 2, 1802.

Lanius, David, and Polly Butt, dau. Regnal Butt, dec.—Feb. 20, 1813.

Lantzford, George, and Betsy Hewett, dau. John Hewett—March 22, 1810.

Lapsley, John, and Mary Armstrong—Dec. 13, 1778.

Larew, Samuel, and Elizabeth Fisher, dau. Anthony Fisher—April 10, 1792.

Lasley (see Lapsley).

Lauderdale, John, and Amelia Wood—Dec. 29, 1795.

Laughland, Dorman, and Mary (Peggy) Kyle —Oct. 20, 1800.

Lavender, George, and Elizabeth Shoemaker, dau William Shoemaker—May 2, 1807.

Lavender Jesse, and Betxy Biglar, dau. Mark Biglar—June 12, 1810.

Ledbetter, Jerry, and Jane Crawford, dau. James Crawford—Jan. 4, 1817.

Lee, Andrew, and Margaret Daniel. Pierce

Daniel, surety—June 25, 1798.

Lee, Jonathan, and Sarah Brickey, dau. Peter Brickey—Sept. 15, 1806.

Lee, Thomas, and Jerushe Hough. Mother, Ruth Hough—Aug 15, 1788.

Lee, William, and Matilda Once—March 11, 1817.

Lee, William (son Zacheriah), and Martha Little, dau. William Little. Both under age—Dec. 23, 1813.

Lee, Zacheriah, Jr., and Agnes Brickey, dau. Peter—May 11, 1813.

Leffel, Anthony, and Polly Miller, dau. Frederick Miller—Sept. 16, 1811.

Leffel, John, and Elizabeth Ovenchain, dau. Samuel Ovenchain—Sept. 26, 1803.

Leffel, John, and Catherine Clapsaddle, dau. George Clapsaddle—May 23, 1805.

Leffler, Jacob, and Peggy Henry, dau. William Henry—April 11, 1822.

Leftwich, John, and Sally Walton, dau. William Walton—Sept. 10, 1802.

Leman, James, and Elizabeth Seaver. Wm. Seaver, surety—March 8, 1796.

Leman, Jacob, and Jenny. Gilliland, dau. James and Susan Gilliland—Jan. 2, 1897.

Lemmon, Andrew, and Patsy Bawler, dau. John Bawler—March 6, 1804.

Lemmon, Conrose, and Nancy Gillelance—April 14, 1801.

Lemmon, David, and Polly Bomgurtner, dau. Frederick Bumgurtner—Sept. 6, 1808.

Lemmon, George, and Nancy Gilliland, dau. George Gilliland—Jan. 17, 1809.

Lemmon, George, and Hannah Williams—Feb. 9, 1811.

Lemmon, Jacob, and Catherine Baker. Henry Baker, surety—June 26, 1811.

Lemmon, Joel, and Margaret James, dau. James James—Nov. 19, 1822.

Lemmon, John, and Mary Kesler, dau. Abram Kesler—Oct. 6, 1822.

Lemmon, Peter, and Elinor Davis, dau. Thomas Davis—May 25, 1818.

Lemmon, Peter, and Leddy Mosely, widow—March 13, 1821.

Leonard, Rufus, and Mary McClorskey—April 3, 1797.

Lentz. Thomas, and Elizabeth Hess—Aug. 24, 1795.

Lewis, Adam, and Margaret Road Heaven—Aug. 31, 1786.

Lewis, Andrew, and Margaret Briant—June 7, 1788.

Lewis, Dr. Andrew, and Maria Walton, dau. William Walton—Oct. 23, 1816.

Lewis, Andrew, Jr., and Elizabeth Madison,

dau. John Madison—May 26, 1778.

Lewis, Richard, and Catherine Jewell, dau. Joseph Jewell—Oct. 21, 1806.

Lewis, Thomas, and Mary Thompson, dau. Joseph Thompson—Aug. 11, 1789. ("Alias Thos. Edward.")

Lewis, Thomas, and Eliza Ann Beale, dau. John Beale—Dec. 4, 1813.

Lewis, Wilson, and Rachel Griffith, dau. Thomas Griffith, dec.—Jan. 26, 1794.

Lilly, Edmund (son Robt. and Frances), and Edy Meadows, dau. Josiah—March 20, 1795.

Linden, Lindon.

Linden, Benjamin, and Mary King—June 10, 1789.

Linden, Jesse, and Jemima King, dau. Robert King—Nov. 2, 1789.

Lindsey, Robert, and Ann Reed, dau. Thomas Reed—Dec. 29, 1804.

Lindsey, Samuel, and Ann McCarroll. John McCarroll, surety—Aug. 13, 1793.

Lindsay, Walter, and Mary M'Calgan—Jan. 17, 1772.

Linkenhoger, Adam, and Margaret Moors, dau. Henry Moore—Oct. 10, 1814.

Linkenhoger, Elias, and Catherine Young, dau. Nicholas Young—May 3, 1803.

Linkenhoger, George, and Elizabeth Stone, John Stone, surety—Jan. 2, 1800.

Linkenhoger, Joseph, and Frances Riddlebarger. John Riddlebarger, surety—Nov. 5, 1800.

Littrel, John, and Catherine Coon, dau. John Coon, Jr.—June 22, 1811.

Littrel, Winstead, and Margaret Bray, dau. John Bray—Aug. 15, 1804.

Little, James, and Eliza Craddock, dau. William Craddock—Aug. 9, 1786.

Little, William, and Margaret Snodgrass—Aug. 16, 1774.

Little, William, and Nancy Craddock, dau. William Craddock, dec.—April 16, 1806.

Littlepage, Samuel B. and Sally Price, dau. Thomas Price—Feb. 9, 1807.

Liveston, John, and Mary Carvin, dau. William Carvin—Dec. 14, 1791.

Lockett, Benjamin, and Frances Sullivan, dau. William Sullivan, dec.—May 6, 1812.

Lockey. James, and Mary Montgomery—Feb. 12, 1796.

Lockey, Thomas, and Susannah Hiney, dau. John Hiney—Dec. 21, 1777.

Logan, Hugh, and Sarah Wood—March 9, 1780.

Logan, Sam, and Sarah Helpinstein—Feb. 24, 1799.

Logan, William, and Agnes M'Cown—Aug. 5,

1775.

Loman, John, and Mary Prichard. Philip Prichard, surety—Jan. 3, 1787.

Long, John, and Nancy Jennings (over 21). Nicholas Long, surety—Dec. 28, 1798.

Long, William, and Polly Redman, dau. William Brown—Aug. 3, 1807.

Looney, Benjamin (son Absolum), and Elizabeth McClure—July 22, 1793.

Looney, David, and Peggy Farrier, dau. Robert Farrier—Jan. 6, 1806.

Looney, John, and Elizabeth Walker, dau. George Walker—March 29, 1804.

Looney, Jonathan, and Mercy Holstine, dau. Henry Holstine—June 3, 1809.

Looney, Joseph, and Nancy Hindrickson, dau. Zaceriah Hendrickson—May 13, 1806.

Looney, Robert (son John), and Catherine Stover, dau. George Stover—Dec. 9, 1809.

Loop, John, and Elizabeth Hypes, dau. Peter Hypes—Jan. 4, 1817.

Love, John, and Sarah Robinson—Sept. 16, 1780.

Lowry, Augustine, and Peggy Miller—Jan. 3, 1821.

Lowry, Moses, and Peggy Miller—Nov. 21, 1803.

Loyd, Levi, and Abby Hale, dau. John and Elizabeth Hale—Jan. 7, 1786.

Luck, William, and Lucy Ann Botts, dau. John Botts—July 8, 1817.

Lukas, David, and Mary Wills. John Lukas, surety—Oct. 11, 1785.

Lutey, Thomas, and .... Evans. Mark Evans, guardian, surety—April 8, 1801.

Lutton, John, and Winny Runnion—Sept. 4, 1783.

Lykills, Thomas, and Mary Kingan—July 14, 1797.

Lykins, Andrew, and Rebekah McNeil—Dec. 11, 1787.

Lyle, James S., and Elizabeth Crutchfield, dau. Robert Crutchfield—Sept. 1820.

Lyons, Ephriam, and Polly Snyder, dau. John Snyder—Feb. 26, 1805.

Lyons, Francis, and Polly McCall, dau. Michael McCall—May 17, 1819.

Lyons, Paul, and Sarah Newton, dau. James Newton—Aug. 4, 1805.

Lypes, Christopher, and Susanna Dill, dau. Henry Dill, dec.—March 24, 1820.

Lypes, Joseph, and Eve Whistler, dau. Henry Whistler—March 20, 1819.

—M—

Madison, Rowland, and Anne Lewis—May 9, 1782.

Maggard, David, and Catherine Houtz—March 18, 1814.

Maggard, Joseph, and Elizabeth Myers, dau. Henry Myers—Dec. 4, 1815.

Mahan, John, and Agnes, and Agnes Leforce—June 21, 1778.

Malcom, James, and Nancy Sands. Wm. Christian Sands, surety—July 7, 1798.

Mallow, Jacob, and Catherine Gutner, dau. Philip Gutner—June 9, 1806.

Mallory, Henry, and Charlotte Bennett, dau. Moses Bennett—Feb. 9, 1808.

Mallory, John, and Polly Coleman, dau. William Coleman—March 4, 1817.

Mallory, Philip, and Elizabeth McCallister, dau. Garland McCallister—Jan. 27, 1817.

Malton, George, and Catherine Triplar, dau. Henry Triplar—Sept. 4, 1810.

Mangus, George, and Susan Graybill, dau. David Graybill—March 31, 1813.

Mangus, Henry, and Jurido Draper, dau. Benjamin Draper—June 20, 1820.

Mangus, Jacob, and Elizabeth Bower, dau. Christopher Bower—Feb. 22, 1819.

Mankpile, Thomas, and Ushey Garrott, dau. George Garrott—April 15, 1807.

Mann, Asa, and Sarah Hair. Moses Mann, surety—March 9, 1780.

Mann, Moses, and Frances Bland, dau. John Bland—Oct. 3, 1778.

Mann, Moses, and Jane Kinkead. Andrew Kinkead, surety—Nov. 11, 1779.

Mann, Samuel, and Margaret Caldwell, dau. William Caldwell—Sept. 7, 1811.

Mann, William, and Nancy Caldwell, dau. John Caldwell—March 10, 1803.

Mapes, Joseph, and Sarah Quarles, dau. David Quarles—Feb. 20, 1791.

Marckle, Benjamin, and Magdalene Peffley, dau. David Peffley—June 12, 1818.

Marckle, Charles, and Polly McClanechan, dau. Wm. McClanechan—Nov. 23, 1805.

Mariam, Frederick, and Barberry Smith. Wm. Smith, surety—April 7, 1787.

Marshall, John, and Elizabeth Allison—Nov. 13, 1778.

Martin, Andrew, and Prudence Robinson, dau. David Robinson—March 28, 1786.

Martin, Isaac, and Elizabeth Kingry, dau. Tobias Kingry—Oct. 16, 1806.

Martin, John, and Milly Lyons—May 9, 1796.

Martin, Jonathan, and Elinor Akins—April 17, 1783.

Martin, Josiah, and Mary Runnels, dau. Joseph Runnels—Aug. 9, 1799.

Martin, Levi, and Peggy Camper. Peter Camper, dec.—Apri 110, 1809.

Martin, Thomas, and Mary A. Boyd, widow of James Boyd—Feb. 19, 1819.

Martin, William, and Elizabeth Leatherdale —Oct. 18, 1785.

Mason, Daniel, and Katy Shortzer—Jan. 17, 1801.

Mason, John, and Betsy Robertson—Dec. 15, 1803.

Mason, Jonathan, and Elizabeth Shatzer, dau. Philip Shatzer—March 11, 1806.

Mason, William, and Isabella Scott—May 28, 1780.

Mason, William, and Eliabeth Goode, dau. Martin Goode—Oct 20, 1794.

Matthews, Isaac, and Martha Henderson, widow of John Henderson—Oct. 3, 1806.

Matthews, John, and Nancy Lyon. Father deceased—Aug. 24. 1809.

Mavey, Benjamin, and Prudence Pryor—July 31, 1786.

Maxey, Caleb, and Sally Lewis, dau. Thomas Lewis—Feb. 6, 1792.

Maxwell, William, and Elizabeth Green, dau. Edward Green—May 13, 1786.

Mayberry, George, and Christeen Kimberline, dau. Paulser and Mary Kimberline— Jan. 5, 1782.

Mays, James, and Sarah Reid, dau. Thomas Reid—Dec. 30, 1795.

Mays, Matthew, and Esther Reid, dau. Thomas Reid—Jan. 8, 1799.

McCafferty, Hugh, and Pricilla Faulconer, dau. Spencer—Feb. 14, 1787.

McCahan, Duncan, and Peggy Richie—Dec. 6, 1799.

McCahan, Malcolm, and Elinor Moss—Jan. 21, 1781.

McCalla, John, and Margaret McBeath, dau. Andrew McBeath—Jan. 1789.

McCallister, Edward, and Mary Dehart. Consent by Wm. and Hannah Yoully—1785.

McCallister, Garland, and Jane Halle—Jan. 27, 1794.

McCallister, Jesse, and

McCallister, John, and Mary Ann Loague— Jan. 7, 1779.

McCallister, John, and Barbara Myers, dau. George Myers—Feb. 8, 1820.

McCallister, Peter, and Elizabeth Mallory, dau. Rodger Mallory—Sept. 22, 1818.

McCallen, Duncan, and Peggy Richey—Dec. 6, 1799. (See McCahan.)

McCallum, Arch D., and Mary Wray, widow of Thomas Wray—Jan. 19, 1809.

McCally, Isaac, and Rebecca Scott, ward of Joseph McCally—Nov. 15, 1819.

McCarney, John, and Jane Davidson, dau.

Wm. Davidson—Jan. 10, 1803.

McCarty, Dennis, and Ann Hammett, dau. David Hammett—Nov. 10, 1791.

McCarty, John, and Leany Woods, dau. Anne Woods—Feb. 10, 1792.

McCaslen, Adam, and Mary Mann—Aug. 11, 1802.

McCaslen, Andrew, and Fancy Green, dau. Edward Green—Dec. 31, 1788.

McCaslin, John, and Sarah Woods, dau. Samuel Woods—March 25, 1818.

McCauley. Campbell, and Mary Harness— Nov. 1, 1787.

McCauley, George, and Pricilla Guliford, dau. Allen Guliford—Sept. 21, 1819.

McCaul, Samuel, and Catherine Zimmerman, dau. William Zimmerman—Feb. 5, 1821.

McClain, James, and Sarah Kyle—Aug. 23, 1785.

McClanahan, Alexander, and Sarah Moore. John Moore, surety—May 5, 1788.

McClanahan, John, and Lucy Walton, dau. William Walton—Feb. 15, 1806.

McClanahan, Robert, and Polly Holstine, dau. Stephen Holstine—Aug. 8, 1805.

McClanahan, William, and Sarah Webb— March 16, 1779.

McClanahan, William, and Margaret Walker, dau. George Walker—May 12, 1818.

McClinock, Alexander, and Sarah Mann— Feb. 6, 1788.

McClung, Arch D., Jr., and Mary Ann Beale, dau. Charles Beale—Jan. 25, 1819.

McClure, Harbert, and Mary McClure, dau. Samuel McClure—Mar. 24, 1795.

McClure, James, and Agnes McClure. John anl Samuel sureties—Sept. 19, 1795.

McClure, Michael, and Nancy Davidson, dau. Thomas Davidson—Nov. 1, 1805.

McClung, Richard, and Molly Crafford, dau. Wm. Crafford—June 27, 1789.

McClure, Robert, and Elizabeth Tygert—Feb. 2, 1799.

McClure, Samuel, and Nancy Pullen—Feb. 11, 1817.

McClure, Thomas, and Jane T. McClure. Samuel McClure, surety (her brother)— March 26, 1778.

McClure, William, and Abby Hughes, dau. William and Franky Hughes—Aug. 20, 1791.

McClure, William, and Margaret Man, dau. Nathan Man, Jan. 4, 1790.

McConnell, Jesse, and Susanna Lockhart, dau. Wm. Lockhart, dec.—April 14, 1807.

McConnell, John, and Catherine Riddle—Jan. 1799.

McConnell, Peter, and Margaret Litten—

March 4, 1817.

McCorkle, Robert, and Mary Holstine, dau. Henry Holstine—Sept. 19, 1789.

McCormick, John, and Ruth Looney, dau. Absolum Looney—May 15, 1790.

McCoun, John, and Elizabeth Telford, dau. James and Catrin Telford—April 14, 1774.

McCoy, Benjamin, and Lucy Arns(Bedford Co.), dau. Edward Arns, dec.—Dec. 23, 1817.

McCoy, Clement, and Joanna Cox, dau. Joseph Cox—Jan. 15, 1814.

McCrary, James, and Rebekah Broadwater—Feb. 11, 1786.

McCrary, John, and Nancy Combs, dau. Gilbert Combs—Oct. 20, 1815.

McCurry, John, and Mary White—Nov. 21, 1781.

McDermed, William, and Anna Stoner, dau. Daniel Stoner—Dec. 4, 1813.

McDonald, Bryan, and Nancy Thomason, dau. John Thomason, dec.—April 26, 1815.

McDonald, Edward, and Mary Rowland, dau. James Rowland—Feb. 19, 1788.

McDonald, John, and Margaret Watkins, dau. Mary Watkins—Dec. 20, 1788.

McDonald, Joseph, and Nancy Smith, dau. Frederick Smith—Feb. 4, 1785.

McDonald, Richard, and Mary Ross. Edward Ross, surety—Jan. 8, 1779.

McDonald, Walter, and Jane McCord. Consent by Mary Henderson—Sept. 6, 1779.

McDonald, Walter, and Margaret Smallwood Aug. 14, 1779.

McDonald, William, and Ann Robinson—Dec. 3, 1779.

McDowell, Thomas, and R...... Little, dau. David Little, dec.—Oct. 2, 1821.

McDowell, William, and Margaret McPherson—Sept. 23, 1786.

McDowell, William A., and Maria H. Harvey, dau. Mathew Harvey—Aug. 24, 1819.

McEleny, Francis, and Susannah Henry. John Henry, surety—Feb. 1, 1781.

McElheney, Robert, and Nancy McKnight, dau. George McKnight—Aug. 12, 1794.

McElwaine, Matthew, and Polly Beard, dau. Thomas Beard—May 22, 1816.

McFaddin, Charles, and Milly Stevens—Sept. 11, 1786.

McFall, James, and Sally Brewser, dau. John Brewster—April 26, 1819.

McFall, John, and Elizabeth McNeal, dau. Hugh McNeal, dec. March 19, 1810.

McFerran, Samuel, and Placy VanMetre—July 13, 1802.

McFerran, John, and Amy Rowland. James Rowland, surety—March 1, 1791.

McFerran, John, and Mary McFerran—Feb. 11, 1779.

McFerran, Thomas, and Mary Carper, dau. Nicholas Carpen—Feb. 1, 1808.

McFerran, Thomas, and Hannah VanMetre, dau. Hetty VanMetre—Jan. 16, 1799.

McFerran, Thomas, and Agnes McFerran, dau. James Aymus McFerran—May 11, 1791.

McGavock, Hugh, and Anna Kent. Consents by Hugh Crocket and Mary Kent—1785.

McGee, David, and Jean Robinson—Sept. 5, 1782.

McGee, and Elisabeth Cox, dau. Allen Cox—Jan. 11, 1789.

McGee, John, and Eliza Cox. Ezekiel Cox, surety—Jan. 12, 1888.

McGeorge, James, and Ann Le force. Samuel Leforce, surety—July 23, 1795.

McGeorge, Samuel, and Ann Scantland, dau. Robert Scantland, dec.—Sept. 17, 1806.

McGeorge, Thomas, and Judith Leforce—July 13, 1784.

McGuire, James, and Anne Goodwin—Sept. 22, 1783.

McHaffey, John, and Jenny Campbell, dau. Robert Campbell—Oct. 23, 1789.

McHenry, John, Peggy Roberts—Nov. 27, 1806.

McIloory, John, and Hetty Shivers, dau. Andrew Shivers—Dec. 7, 1811.

McIver, John, and Polly Kyle Trenor, dau. James Trenor—Dec. 29, 1809.

McKenny, James, and Elizabeth Brickey—Peter Brickey, surety—Dec. 1, 1801.

McKenney, John, and Nelly Larkin. Hugh L. Larkin, surety—Jan. 7, 1800.

McKnight, James, and Nancy Lackey, dau. James Lackey—Jan. 1, 1821.

McKnight, John, and Martha Lackey, dau. James Lackey—Nov. 15, 1806.

McMahan, James, and Rachel Colvert. Robert Colvert, surety—Dec. 1, 1788.

McMullen, Andrew, and Polly Finney, dau. Timothy Finney—Feb. 4, 1794.

McMullen, Edward, and Sarah Read, dau. Wm. and Rutha Read—March 11, 1787.

McMullen, James, and Jane Robinson, dau. James and Elizabeth Robinson—March 14, 1788.

McMullen, Matthew, and Polly Wysong, dau. Fiatt Wysong—Aug. 18, 1801.

McMullen, Robert, and Esther Beals, dau. Jonathan Beals—Oct. 11, 1813.

McMurray, John, and Elizabeth McClelan.

Wm. McClelan, surety—Oct. 4, 1785.

McMurtry, John, and Ann Campbell. John Campbell, surety—Oct. 28, 1779.

McNeil, Jonathan (son Neil and Margaret McNeil), and Jane McCord—Sept. 6, 1779.

McNutt, Joseph, and Peggy Boyd, widow—March 9, 1807.

McPherson, Bastin, and Elizabeth McPherson, dau. Alexander McPherson—May 13, 1789.

McRoberts, Alexander, and Nancy Hiland—May 3, 1784.

McRoberts, John, and Sarah McClanahan, dau. Francis McClanahan—April 12, 1770.

McRoberts, John, and Eunice Crawford—Aug. 5, 1793.

McWhorter, ..., and Catherine Aughleman, dau. Jacob—March 8, 1806.

Meador, Thomas, and Sarah Cooper, dau. Dabney Cooper—Jan. 17, 1806.

Meadows, Jacob, and Polly Ovengton—June 7, 1795.

Means, Hugh, and Sarah Snodgrass. Consents by Hugh Means and John Snodgrass—Aug. 19, 1796.

Melling, William, and Catherine Vinyard, dau. Jacob Vinyard—Aug. 23, 1816.

Melling, William, and Margaret Wertz, dau. Wm. Wertz—Feb. 21, 1816.

Mellon, Andrew, and Margaret Scott, dau. Nathan Scott—April 3, 1814.

Melone, John, and Elizabeth Moore, dau. Thomas Moore—Dec. 18, 1816

Mellow, Michael, Jr., and Charlotte Gortner, dau. Philip Gortner—March 12, 1816.

Merritt, Samuel, and Mary Keith—July 30, 1817.

Middlecroff, David, and Polly Hess, dau. Jacob Hess—April 8, 1806.

Middlecroff, John, Jr., and Nancy Calbreath, dau. John Calbreath—Aug. 16, 1811.

Middlecroff, John, and Elizabeth Bolinger, widow—Dec. 17, 1812. ,

Milenor, Lee, and Mildred Harris, dau. John Harris—Dec. 27, 1813.

Miles, Thomas, and Elizabeth Engard, dau. William EngardROct. 7, 1815.

Miller, Benjamin, and Christina Townsley, wid John, and dau. Nicholas Markley—Aug. 3 1815.

Miller, Benjamin, and Elinor Forguson, "orphan of Andrew Forguson"—Dec. 10, 1816.

Miller, Benjamin, and Mary Fields, dau. John Fields, dec.—Oct. 12, 1812.

Miller, Frederick, and Elizabeth Carvin, dau. Wm. Carvin—May 27, 1805.

Miller, George (son of John), and Melinda Breedlove, dau. Isaac Breedlove—Dec. 12, 1820.

Miller, George, and Sarah Niday, dau. Abraham—Jan 2, 1822.

Miller, Henry, and Polly Vans—Sept. 1, 1821.

Miller, Henry, and Elizabeth Breedlove, dau. Isaac Breedlove—Feb. 22, 1821.

Miller, Jacob, and Catherine Uring, dau. Jacob Uring—Oct. 4, 1810.

Miller, Jacob, and Elizabeth Ritter, dau. Michael Ritter—June 11, 1805.

Miller, Jacob, and Catherine Gurtner. Philip Gurtner, surety—June 9, 1806.

Miller, John, and Sarah Carter—Aug. 15, 1785.

Miller, Joseph, and Betsy Allen, dau. Hugh Allen—Feb. 17, 1796.

Miller, Joseph, and Elizabeth McFalls, dau. Wm. McFalls—Sept. 6, 1818.

Miller, Martin, and Polly Crepoe, dau. Mathias Crepoe—June 13, 1807.

Miller, Samuel, and Mary Armentrout, dau. George Armentrout—Dec. 28, 1819.

Miller, Thomas, and Mary Clark—Oct. 1, 1780.

Millerons, Christopher, and Abagail Wall—April 8, 1785

Millerons, David, and Elizabeth Moulds. Jacob Moulds, surety—Aug. 8, 1797.

Millhollin, Patrick, and Hannah Pence, dau. Elizabeth Pence—May 18, 1816.

Millhillin, Thomas, and Martha Wright, dau. Peter Wright—March 5, 1817.

Milling, David, and Nancy Nafe. John Naff, surety—Aug. 4, 1800.

Millison, Henry, and Elizabeth Wall dau. Conrad Wall—May 29, 1780.

Mills, David, and Nancy Hayes. John Hayes, surety—April 4, 1797.

Mills, John, and Martha Ewing, dau. Robert Ewing (of Bedford)—Jan. 14, 1772.

Mills, James, and Elizabeth Phipps, dau. Josiah Phipps—March 24, 1784.

Mills, William, and Sarah Lemox (over 21). Wm. Lemox, surety, her brother—May 20, 1788.

Miltebarger, William, and Peggy Francisco, dau. Michael Francisco—Oct. 29, 1802.

Mingas, John, Jr., and Hannah Ronck, dau. George Ronck—Feb. 5, 1803.

Minor, William A., and Jane Cooper, dau. Charles Cooper—May 3, 1819.

Minnick, Adam, and Mary Hill—March 25, 1797.

Minnick, Jacob, and Polly Leader—April 29, 1795.

Minnick, John, and Mary Moyers. Peter Minnick, surety—Jan 27, 1795.

Minnick, John, and Sarah Unrue, dau. John

—33—

Unrue—Nov., 1822.

Minnick, Michael, and Rebecca Stever, dau. George Stever—Feb. 4, 1821.

Minnick, Peter, and Katherine Wortmiller—Aug. 1, 1792.

Minore, Archellus D., and Elizabeth Combs, dau. Gilbert Combs—Oct. 12, 1818.

Mitchell, David and Susanna Buser, dau. Jacob Buser—May 14, 1812.

Mitchell, James, and Anna Walton, dau. William Walton—March 23, 1811.

Mitchell, John, and Elizabeth King. Thomas King surety—May 14, 1794.

Mitchell, John, and Sally Shahan, dau. John Shahan—Aug. 11, 1802.

Mitchell, John. and Nancy Beard dau. Thomas Beard,dec.—Dec. 26, 1810.

Mitchell, Samuel, Jr., and Sarah E. Booth, dau. William Booth—March 4, 1814.

Mitchell, Thomas, and Margaret Snider, dau Henry Snider—Dec. 10, 1817.

Mitchell, William, and Sarah Hawkins—July 23, 1795.

Monicle, George, and Lucy Bandy—Aug. 9, 1797.

Monroe, William, and Sahar Centz, dau. Jacob Centz——May 26, 1820.

Montgomery, James, and Elizabeth McFerran. Samuel McFerran surety—Sept. 13, 1792.

Montgomery, Joseph, and Jane McFerran, dau. Samuel McFerran—Aug. 13, 1816.

Montgomery, Robert, and Sarah Skidmore (Over 21), dau. James Skidmore of Rock-Rockbridge—Nov. 22, 1796.

Moony, Edward, and Frances Carter, dau. John and Sarah Nutter—March 17, 1794.

Moody, Martin, and Martha Guthrie, dau. Wm. Guthrie, dec.—Oct. 16, 1810.

Mooman, Christian, and Catherine Snider. Peter Snider, surety—Jan. 25, 1800.

Mooman, William, and Mary Burkholder, dau Isaac Burkholder—Dec. 1, 1805.

Moomaw, John, and Sophia Snider, dau. Peter Snider—Feb. 2, 1802.

Moomaw, Philip, and Katherine Biglar. Mark Biglar surety—Dec. 14, 1805.

Moore, David, and Isabella Harston. John Moore, surety—Sept. 11, 1793.

Moore, Hugh, and Anne Allen, dau. Hugh Allen—Aug. 13, 1807.

Moore, James, and Elizabeth Harrison, dau. Stephen Harrison—Oct. 2, 1807.

Moore, Levi, and Margaret Salmon, dau. Jacob Salmon—Oct. 21, 1807.

Moore, Samuel, and Mary Smiley, dau. Walter Smiley, dec.—March 3, 1814.

Moore, Thomas, and Martha Woods. Joseph Woods,surety—Feb. 14, 1795.

Moore, Thomas, and Elizabeth McCreary—June 30, 1785.

Moore, William (son of Stephen), and Elizabeth Patterson. Wm. Patterson, surety—Dec. 24, 1798.

Moran, John, and Mary Walker, dau. John Walker—April 7, 1787.

Morris, Benjamin (of Rockbridge), and Elizabeth Catron, dau. Robert—Sept. 29, 1788.

Morris, James, and Ruth Reed, dau. Wm. Reed. John Morris, surety—Feb. 14, 1789.

Morris, John, and Jane Scott, dau. John Scott—Oct. 2, 1789.

Morris, Joseph, and Elizabeth Speers, dau. Joseph Speers—Sept. 29, 1788.

Morris, Patrick, and Sarah Bellamy—July 27, 1790.

Morris, William, and Mary Barns. Leonard Robinson, her guardian, surety—June 28, 1798.

Morris, William, and Margaret McClintick, dau. William—March 25, 1788.

Morrow, James, and Margaret Mahan. Patrick Mahan, surety—April 8, 1779.

Morton, James and Mary Mayes, dau. James Mayes—Oct. 9, 1822.

Moses, James, and Polly Taylor, dau. Jacob Taylor—July 25, 1815.

Moses, John, and Jane Wood, dau Zacheriah Wood—Dec. 10, 1817.

Moses, Mann, and Jane Kinkhead—Nov. 11, 1779.

Moyers, Adam, and Catherine Jones—Dec. 26, 1792.

Moyers, Conrad, and Catherine Miller—Feb. 8, 1794.

Moyers, David, and Polly Grainor, dau. George Grainor—1821.

Moyers, Henry, and Mary Beckner, dau. Nicholas Beckner—Dec. 30, 1790.

Moyers, John and Catherine Niday, dau. David Niday—Dec. 18, 1805.

Muldrough, Hugh, and Jean Frazier, dau. Mary Frazier—Sept., 1781.

Mupires, James, and Jane Muldwick—Jan. 9, 1779.

Murphy, George, and Sally Augerman, dau. Jacob Augerman—Aug. 8, 1807.

Murphy, John, and Mary Litteral, dau. Richard—May 4, 1813.

Murphy, Robert, and Martha McNeil. Hugh McNeil, surety—Oct. 8, 1783.

Murphy, Thomas, and Susanna Kenning, widow of John—Oct. 12, 1807.

Murray, James, and Barbara Hammon—July 17, 1799.

Murray, John, and Polly Keefauvor—May 13, 1822.

Muse, John, and Sarah Rivier, dau. Johnson Rivier—Jan. 20, 1803.

Muse, William (son of John), and Fanny Blackaly, dau. Wm.—Dec. 28, 1809.

Myers, John, and Katherine Niday. David Niday, surety—Dec. 18, 1805.

Myers, John, and Mary Moore, dau. Henry Moore—Jan. 13, 1812.

Myers, John, and Elizabeth Britz, dau. John Britz—May 2, 1815.

Myers, Samuel, and Elizabeth Smith. Jacob Myers, surety—May 11, 1795.

—N—

Nace, George, and Elizabeth Staley, dau. Jacob Staley, dec.—Oct. 11, 1814.

Name, Henry, and Anne Frantz, dau. Henry Frantz—March 30, 1822.

Nail, John, and Mary Ockerman, dau. Jacob Ockerman—Feb. 21, 1803.

Nash, Gabriel, and Elizazbeth McClanahan, dau. Elisha McClanahan—May, 8, 1816.

Nautz, Peter, and Mary Pryor. Joseph Pryor, surety—March 9, 1801.

Nave, John, and Susanna Gray, dau. James Gray—Oct. 6, 1795.

Nave, Peter, and Mary I. Noftzinger, dau. Samuel Noftzinger—Oct. 9, 1820.

Neal, William, and Jane Dunbar. Consent by Mary Dunbar—Oct. 7, 1794.

Neely, James, and Jane Neely, dau. John Neely—Nov. 2, 1802.

Neely, Robert. Sr., and Nancy Haden, dau. Sharlot Haden—April 7, 1794.

Neely, William, and Elizabeth Gholson, dau. Anthony Gholson—Nov. 27, 1787.

Neidy, Abraham, and Susanna Snodgrass—June 26, 1800.

Neidy, John, and Catherine Wall. David Neidy, surety—June 12, 1787.

Neighbors, Fleming, and Elizabeth James, dau. John James—June 8, 1819.

Neighbors, John, and Sophia Henry, dau. William Henry—Nov. 5, 1820.

Neinanger, Jacob, and Rebecca Reis—June 3, 1799.

Nelson, Andrew. and Martha Wilson, dau. Thomas Wilson—Nov. 30, 1790.

Nevill, John, and Mary Lemmon, dau. Christian Lemmon—March 18, 1812.

Newanger, Jacob, and Rebecca Read—July 4, 1799.

Newcom, John, and Catherine Mennich, dau.

Benjamin Mennich—Feb. 21, 1807.

Newman, Benjamin, and Mary Kind, dau. William Kind—Jan. 6, 1815.

Newman, George, and Nancy Brunk, dau. John Brunk, dec.—April 22, 1811.

Newman, John, and Susanna Goff, dau Ambrose Goff—Nov. 12, 1803.

Newell, Thomas, and Nancy Gillespy, dau. Simon Gillespy—Oct. 29, 1802.

Newton, Jacob, and Betsy Snider, dau. John Snider—May 8, 1811.

Newton, Peter, and Sally Falls, dau. Peter Falls—Nov. 18, 1805.

Nicely, George, and Sarah Circle, dau. Peter Circle—June 3, 1809.

Nicely, Jacob, and Magdalene Circle, dau. Peter Circle—Dec. 19, 1798.

Nicewonger, John, and Betsy Circle, dau. Peter Circle—Sept. 23, 1807.

Nicewonger, Samuel, and Elinor Dillon, dau. James Dillon—Sept. 10, 1807.

Niday, David, and Nancy Scott. Joseph Scott, surety—Sept. 4, 1798.

Niday, John, and Margaret Huff, dau. Jacob Huff—March 13, 1818.

Nigh, Peter, and Elizabeth Seagle—Aug. 15, 1796.

Noble, David, and Susanna Emmons—Feb. 4, 1784.

Nofsinger, David, and Polly Horn—July 1, 1799.

Nofsinger, Joseph, and Mary Harshbarger, dau. Samuel Harshbarger—Sept. 14, 1812.

Nofsinger, Peter, and Mary Pettinger—June 2, 1799.

Nofsinger, Samuel, and Mary Hiner, dau. John Hiner—Aug. 5, 1791.

Noftzinger, Jacob, and Elizabeth Snider, dau. Mathias Snider—Aug. 11, 1807.

Noftzinger, John, and Susanna Gish, dau. David Gish—April 3, 1814.

Noke, Stockley, and Margery Crawford, dau. James Crawford—Feb. 11 1801.

Noonin, Patrick, and Sarah Hawkins, dau. Thomas Hawkins—Jan. 31, 1789.

Nowell, John, and Catherine Griffith, dau. John Griffith. Wm. Nowell, surety—Sept. 24, 1791.

Nowell, Nathan, and Nancy Carvin, dau. William Carvin—March 19, 1794.

Nowell, William, and Elizabeth Hannah—June 11, 1799.

Nowell, William, and Mary Payne. Dudley Payne, surety—Sept. 8, 1801.

Nowell, Young, and Margaret Miller—Aug. 12, 1800.

Nox, William, and Anna Reed, dau. William

Reed—Jan. 17, 1789.

Jugent, James, and Mary Jenkins—May, 1797.

Jugent, John, and Elizabeth Mifford—May 16, 1797.

Jull William, and Mary Dennis—April 1, 1779.

Jutter, Walter, and Elizabeth Craige, dau. Samuel Craige—Dec. 8, 1821.

—O—

O'Brian, Thomas, and Jane Coffee—Jan. 17, 1787.

Ochtree, James, and Jemima Caldwell—Sept. 19, 1800.

Ochtree, John, and Catey McCluer. Samuel McCluer, surety—Jan. 31, 1797.

O'Hair, Michael, and Elinor Hawks—June 10, 1783.

Old, Anderson, and Elizabeth Haines, dau. Henry Haines—March 6, 1821.

Old, Charles, and Mary Snodgrass, dau. Joseph Snodgrass, dec.—June 22, 1815.

Old, John and Hannah Bise, dau. John Bise —Nov. 22, 1810.

Olinger, John, and Ursula Doble, dau. Joseph Doble—June 17, 1820.

Oliver, John, and Elizabeth Hill, dau. William Hill—March 26, 1821.

O'Neal, Felix, and Nancy Gish dau. John Gish—April 24, 1807.

Orndorf, Jesse, and Betsy Cashman, dau. Martin Cashman—Dec. 29, 1803.

Osborne, Henry, and Charlotte Haley, "an orphan" of William Haley—Feb. 27, 1790.

Osborne, Robert, and Eliz. Lafoan—Oct. 28, 1784.

Otey, Thomas, and Elizabeth Simpson—April 21, 1795.

Otey, Walter, and Polly Walton—June 28, 1800.

Outinrude, John, and Margaret McBeath, dau. Andrew McBeath—Jan. 1789.

Ovenchain, Daniel, and Hannah Marquart, dau. Philip Marquart—Feb. 1, 1803.

Ovenchain, Jacob, and Polly Ovenchain, dau. Rinholt Ovenchain—March 21, 1820.

Ovenchain, Peter, and Christina Beckner, dau. Jonathan Beckner—Dec. 21, 1812.

Ovenchain, Rhineholt, and Polly Hewett, dau. John Hewett—Aug. 12, 1807.

Ovenchain, Samuel, and Martha Toler— March 2, 1821.

Ovenchain, William, and Sarah Foster, widow of Michael—Feb. 6, 1813.

Ovenchain, William, and Susanna Snider, dau. John Snider—Sept. 7, 1816.

Overholster, Christian, and Catherine Fizer— July 30, 1798.

Owens, Barnett (son of David), and Margaret Peatross, dau. Mathew Peatross— July 7, 1789.

Owens, David, and Rachel Henry, dau. Wm. Henry—May 12, 1815.

Owens, Thomas, and Elizabeth Simpkins, dau. Wm. Simpkins—Aug. 29, 1815.

Owens, William ,and Jane Smiley, dau. William Smiley—May 12, 1811.

Oyler, Jacob, and eggy Shamaker. Peter Shamaker surety—Feb. 15, 1796.

—P—

Painter, Barney, and Margaret Smith—Aug. 10, 1819.

Painter, Conrad, and Barbara Moulds. Jacob Moulds, surety—Dec. 12, 1797.

Painter, Jacob, and Mary Magdalene Etzler, dau. George Etzler—Sept. 7, 1807.

Painter, John, and Sarah Bean, dau. Joseph Bean—Aug. 12, 1806.

Painter, John, and Susanna Harshbarger, dau. Christian Harshbarger—Oct. 5, 1819.

Painter, Joshua, and Mary Slaughter, dau. Griff Slaughter—Oct. 12, 1806.

Painter, Peter, and Rosanna Bean, dau. Joshua Bean—Oct. 22, 1811.

Pannell, Joseph, and Peggy Jones, dau. Joseph Jones—Nov. 2, 1818.

Parris, Parrish, Parish

Parris, Charles, and Polly Rifley, dau. George Rifley—Sept. 20, 1819.

Parrish, Colin, and Elizabeth Lee, dau Zacheriah Lee—Sept. 23, 1808.

Parish, Samuel, and Elizabeth Shewsberry, widow of Dabney—Sept. 23, 1808.

Parker, Hugh, and Margaret Knox, dau. Elisha Knox—Sept. 14, 1807.

Parker, Thomas, and Betsy Hawkins, dau. John and Elizabeth Hawkins—March 25, 1798.

Parrott, John, and Catherine Mifford—Dec. 31, 1801.

Pate, Edwin, and Mary Crawford, dau. James Crawford—April 6, 1789.

Pate, John, and Janet Crawford, dau. Peter Crawford—Oct. 20, 1792.

Patterson, George, and Catherine Smyth, dau. Frederick Smyth—Dec. 22, 1785.

Patterson, Moses, and Jane Humphrey, dau. Margaret Humphrey—Aug. 8, 1816.

Patterson, Robert (son of William), and Elizabeth Porter, dau. Samuel Porter—Oct. 15, 1804.

Patterson, William, and Letis Taylor, dau. Thomas Taylor—July 14, 1789.

Patterson, William, and Rebekah Persinger,

dau Henry Persinger—March 22, 1813.

Paul, James, and Mary McKnight, dau. George McKnight—Feb. 19, 1790.

Paul, John, and Jean M'Colough, dau. Jannet McColough—June 28, 1787.

Pauley, Edward, and Hester Carleton. Henry Carleton, surety—March 5, 1787.

Paup, John, and Sarah Pitzer, dau. John Pitzer—Jan. 22, 1807.

Pauper, John, and Dolly Kessler, dau. John Kessler—Dec. 19, 1820.

Paupes, John, and Cate Howry. Michael Howry, surety—Nov. 20, 1786.

Paupey, Elijah, and Margaret Rhinehart, dau. Peter Rhinehart—Feb. 6, 1816.

Paxton, James, and Catherine Jordon, dau. John Jordon—June 7, 1817.

Paxton, John, and Elizabeth Logan, dau. John Logan. Thomas Paxton, surety—May 29, 1789.

Paxton, Thomas, and Polly (Mary) Barclay. Hugh Barclay, surety—July 5, 1774.

Paxton, William, and Hannah Abbott, dau. Thomas Abbott—Oct. 6, 1813.

Peas, Thomas, and Phebe Martin, dau. Johnson Martin—Aug. 11, 1809.

Pearcy, Edward, and Peggy Kelly, dau. George Kelly, dec., and Mary Kelly—Jan. 11, 1803.

Pearie, James, and Elinor Dennis—March 8, 1777.

Pearie, Thomas, and Margaret Dennis—Jan. 31, 1781.

Pearson, Palmer, and Margaret Combs, dau. Gilbert Combs—Sept. 4, 1817.

Peck, Adam, and Mary Green. Edward Green, surety—June 24, 1777.

Peck, Adam, and Elizabeth Shirkey—June 24, 1777.

Peck, Adam, and Catherine Stever, dau. George Stever—Dec. 18, 1804.

Peck, Jacob, and Leney Givens, dau. Daniel Givens—Feb. 2, 1802.

Peck, Jacob, and Patsy Walker, dau. John Walker—April 6, 1818.

Peck, Jacob, and Jane Waggoner, dau. James Waggoner, dec.—Aug. 21, 1815.

Peck, John H. and Mary M. McCrery, dau. John McCrery, dec.—Oct. 6, 1811.

Peck, Joseph, and Susanna Franklin—Aug. 29, 1792.

Peck, Lewis, and Polly Jones, dau. Allen Jones—Dec. 24, 1811.

Pedan, James, and Nancy Willson, dau. Sam'l Willson—April 29, 1784.

Peeling, John, and Elizabeth Tate, widow of Nathaniel G. Tate—Oct. 24, 1811.

Pefley, David, and Mary Graybill, dau. Daniel Graybill—June 15, 1815.

Pefley, Henry, and Susanna Bondrager—April 20, 1797.

Pefley, Samuel, and Nancy Barndrager, dau. David and Susanna Barndrager—Aug. 16, 1799.

Penn, Jacob and Elizabeth Trim—April 13, 1799.

Pennhead, Alexander, and JeaKnne Lemore. Consent by Hannah Lemore—Oct. 9, 1796.

Pennington, John, and Elizabeth Addkins. Consent by mother, Mary Addkins—Jan. 14, 1793.

Perrey, Thomas, and Elliner Smith, "over 21" —April 5, 1798.

Persinger, Andrew, and Elizabeth Sticklemen, dau. John Sticklemen—July 24, 1811.

Persinger, George, and Elizabeth Bremmer, dau. Conrad Bremmer—Dec. 23, 1802.

Persinger, Jacob, and Mary imberland—Nov. 14, 1778.

Persinger, Jacob, and Margaret Reed, dau. William Reed—Oct. 1797.

Persinger, Jacob, and Catherine Stull, father dec.—Dec. 23, 1803.

Persinger, John, and Elizabeth Patterson, dau. Wm.—Aug. 27, 1816.

Persinger, John, and Elizabeth Kimberline— Nov. 10, 1778.

Persinger, John, and Catherine Brown, dau. George Brown—July 3, 1817.

Persinger, William, and Barbara Trustlee— Nov. 28, 1815.

Peterman, George, and Susanna Kifman, dau. Peter—Dec. 1, 1803.

Peterman, Jacob, and Susanna Cassner, widow John—May 12, 1802.

Peterman, Jacob, and Rosanna Kish, dau. Christian Kish—Nov. 23, 1802.

Peters, Abraham, and Anna Critz, dau. George Critz, dec.—Dec. 12, 1807.

Peters, Daniel, and Elizabeth Eller, dau. Jacob Eller—Dec. 7, 1814.

Petty, Abner, and Ely Leargin, widow of James—Dec. 3, 1819.

Petty, Abner, and Mary Smith, dau. Absolum Smith—June 11, 1805.

Pettygrew, James, and Sarah Kinney, dau. John Kinney, dec—Feb. 12, 1817.

Phillips, Jacob, and Mary Eve Whitmer, dau. John Whitmer—April 1, 1807.

Phillips, Samuel, and Nancy Mitchell, dau. Rev. Edward Mitchell—Nov. 10, 1805.

Phillips, John, and Else Livesnston, dau. William and Rebecca—July 27, 1796.

Phillips, Thomas, and Sarah Lemon, dau.

Fredrk Lemon—May 11, 1801.

Pile,, John, and Patsy Allen, dau. Hugh Allen—June 27, 1801.

Pitman, Robert, and Christinah Craft, dau. Philip Craft—April 16, 1821.

Pitzer, Abraham (son of John), and Polly Poage (over 21)—Sept. 20, 1798.

Pitzer, Bernard, and Jane Kyle, dau. Joseph Kyle—Aug. 10, 1798.

Pitzer, Davidson, and Amanda Poage—Jan. 28, 1821.

Pitzer, Frederick, and Nancy Kimberling, dau. Palser Kimberling—May 22, 1798.

Pitzer, George, and Elizabeth Kyle, dau. Wm. Kyle—Feb. 26, 1805.

Pitzer, John, and Margaret Little—Jan. 14, 1794.

Pitzer, William (son of John), and Rebecca Kimberling, dau. Palser Kimberling—Feb. 15, 1804.

Platt, Henry, and Rebecca Speakle, dau. Lawrence Speagle—Dec. 4, 1820.

Plymale, Anthony, and Batha Bone (Boan?). John Bowen, surety—Jan. 11, 1789.

Plymale. John, and Jane Tweley. Anthony Plymale, surety—Oct. 31, 1791.

Poage, Poague.

Poage, George, and Polly Kyle, dau. Wm. Kyle. Barclay Kyle, surety—Nov. 16, 1802.

Poage, John and Jane Kyle, dau. Wm. Kyle—Nov. 16, 1802.

Poage, John, and Catherine Sheets, ward John Butts, surety—June 20, 1807.

Poage, John, and Margaret Polk, dau. Joseph Polk—Aug. 17, 1811.

Poage, Samuel, and Agnes Kyle—Oct. 25, 1779.

Poage, Thomas, and Mary Dagger, dau. Peter Dagger—May 13, 1817.

Poage, William, and Elizabeth Franklin, dau. Nathan Franklin—Dec. 17, 1806.

Poage, William, and Susanna Boughan, dau. Joseph and Nancy Boughan—Nov. 16, 1799.

Polk, Joseph, and .... Clark—Dec. 13, 1800.

Polk, William, and Mary Goodwin (aged 21), dau. Daniel Goodwin—1797.

Pont, John, and Dolly Bishop, dau. Jacob Bishop—April 27, 1813.

Poppa, Jacob, and Christina Snider, dau. Jacob Snider—Sept. 22, 1811.

Porter, Isaac, and Margaret Grammer, dau. Joseph Grammer—March 19, 1812.

Porter, James, and Catherine Hughes—Feb. 12, 1796.

Porter, Samuel, and Sarah Johnston—April 2, 1788.

Potts, Nathan (son of John) and Hannah Shannon—Oct. 4, 1772.

Potts, ..., and Jane Culberson—July 8, 1772.

Pratt, James, and Sarah Litteral—July 30, 1799.

Pratt, John, and Nancy Mansfiel—Dec. 26, 1801.

Preston, George, and Jean Luney, dau. Joseph Luney—May 14, 1787.

Preston, Robert, and Elizabeth Amyx, dau. Samuel Amyx—June 9, 1810.

Preston, William, and Carolina Hancock. George Hancock, surety—March 28, 1802.

Price, Christopher M., and Harriet Kyle, dau. William Kyle—Dec. 3, 1818,

Price, Jacob, and Sophia Price, dau. Thomas Price—Oct. 6, 1813.

Price, William, and Rechel Tillery, dau. John Tillery—March 23, 1778.

Prince, John, and Rebekah Brown, dau. Thomas Brown—Oct. 30, 1811.

Prothers, Thomas, and Hannah Miles, dau. Bartholomew Miles—Aug. 11, 1785.

Pruit, Obediah, and Chrizziah Jarvis—March 25, 1799.

Prunk, John, and Nancy Smith, dau. William Smith—March 11, 1814.

Pryor, Thornton, and Polly Nance, dau. Thomas Nance. Joseph Pryor, surety—Jan. 20, 1802.

Pullen, John, and Elizabeth Bennett, dau. Moses Bennett—April 11, 1798.

Putman, John, and Mary LUong. Henry Putman, surety—Jan. 1, 1794.

—Q—

Quarles, William, and Polly Lamb, dau Archd and Pollie Lamb—Jan. 12, 1788.

Quincy, Robert, and Elizabeth Gwaltney, dau. Michael Gwaltney—Sept. 17, 1807.

Quirk Thomas, and Jane Kent—Sept. 9, 1783.

—R—

Radford, John, and Harriett Kennerly, dau. Samuel—Dec. 23, 1806.

Rador, Abraham, and Barbara Kissler, dau. John Kissler—June 6, 1814.

Rador, George, and Susanna Kessler, dau. John Kessler—Dec. 20, 1819.

Raburn, Reyburn, Raeburn.

Raeburn, John, and Elizabeth Green. James Raeburn, surety—Aug. 27, 1782.

Raeburn, Joseph N., and Polly B. George—April 14, 1818.

Raeburn, Thomas, and Mary Wood, dau.

Arch Wood. James Raeburn, surety—May 13, 1789.

Rakes, Caleb, and Polly Ball (Bane?), dau. Henry, dec.—Sept. 21, 1822.

Ramsey, Hugh, and Frances Shepherd, dau. Dubarton Shepherd—March 21, 1803.

Ramsey, Samuel, and Elizabeth Allen—Feb. 20, 1797.

Ray, Barton, and Polly Kessler, dau. John Kessler—Oct. 24, 1816.

Ray, Lewis, and Betsy Zeglar, dau. Paul Zeglar—Jan. 4, 1812.

Read Reed.

Read, Alexander, and Rebeccah Camron—Sept. 18, 1780.

Read, John, and Ruth Thorp. William Thorp, surety—Feb. 25, 1800.

Read, John, and Hannah Francisco—June 15, 1797.

Read, John, and Janet McMurrey, dau. William McMurrey—Aug. 8. 1788.

Read, Patrick, and Mary Boyle—April 2, 1788.

Read, Samuel, and Lucy Faulconer. Hugh Faulkner, suret—Jan. 27, 1794.

Read, Toomey (under age), and Rebecca McMahan—Nov. 23, 1788. Toomey, son of Michael.

Read, William, and Prudence Rowland, dau. James Rowland, dec. Dec. 25, 1805.

Reed, William, and Mary Ryan—Feb. 3, 1779.

Reed, William, and Fanny Barnes, dau. Thomas Barnes—Jan. 15, 1802.

Reader, Abraham ,and Jemima Howell, dau. George Howell—Dec. 28, 1802.

Rector. John, and Chloe McPherson, dau. Richard McPherson—Sept. 29, 1786.

Redman, John, and Christinah Deal, dau. Peter Deal—Aug. 9. 1804.

Redman, Stephen, and Nancy Clemmons—March 13, 1799.

Redman, William, and Mary Brown. William Brown, surety—Sept. 9, 1800.

Reese, David and Greesay Loague, dau. Samuel (Poague?)—Jan. 20, 1779.

Reevis, Benjamin, and Catherine Frantz, dau. Daniel Frantz—Aug. 14, 1811.

Resque, see Risque.

Reynolds, Bennett S. and Pricilla Caldwell, dau. William—Nov. 11, 1822.

Reynolds, James, and Susannah Trout, dau. Jacob Trout—1799.

Reynolds, James, and Susanna Hughes, dau. Thomas Hughes—July 30, 1793.

Reynolds, Larkin, and Hannah Furguson, dau. Andrew Furguson—March 2, 1806.

Reynolds, Lewis, anl Mary Garwood, dau. Joseph Garwood—Oct. 10, 1818.

Reynolds, Robert, and Magdalena Gross, widow Jacob—Nov. 29, 1809.

Reynolds, Silas, and Jane Greenlee. William Greenlee, surety—June 8, 1797.

Reynolds, Thomas, and Sahar Caldwell. Hugh Caldwell, surety—Dec. 16, 1796.

Reynolds, Thomas, and Mary Bennett, dau. Moses Bennett—April 25, 1797.

Reynolds, Thomas, and Mary Love. Consent by Jean Love—March, 1797.

Reynolds, William, and Amey Elder—Dec. 19, 1786.

Reynolds, William L., and Betsy Campbell, dau. Edward Campbell—Nov. 24, 1819.

Reynolds, William E., and Elizabeth Looney—June 21, 1817.

Rice, David, and Polly Eakin, dau. Nathin Eakin—July 15, 1806.

Rice, William, and Anna Moyers, dau. George Moyers—Nov. 5, 1820.

Rich, David, and Susanna Harshbarger, dau. C......—Sept. 15, 1816.

Richards, Ambrose, and Milly Johnston—July 18, 1797.

Richards, Richard, and Sarah Richards. Richard Richards, surety. Richard Rains, grandfather—June 12, 1802.

Richards, William, and Martha Richards. Richard Richars, surety—Sept. 29, 1801.

Richardson, Green, and Leah Eddington, dau. Philip—Feb. 5, 1821.

Richardson, Samuel, and Margaret Vineyard, dau. Christian Vineyard—Jan. 26, 1820.

Richardson, William S., and Damarus Booth, dau. Alexander Booth—May 18, 1820.

Richeson, Jonathan, and Mary Horn, dau. Charles Horn—Oct. 28, 1816.

Richey, James, and Mary Beckner, dau Abraham Beckner, dec.—Jan. 12, 1818.

Richey, John, and Catherine Harley, widow of James—Nov. 14, 1796.

Riddell, John, and Anna Harshbarger, dau. Christian—June 26, 1820.

Riddlebarger, David, and Ann Linkenharger, dau. Elias—Dec. 17, 1816.

Riddlebarger, Samuel, and Sarah Compton. John Riddlebarger, surety—Sept. 1, 1794.

Rife, Samuel, and Racheal Nicewonger, dau. John Nicewonger—Nov. 17, 1810.

Riffey, John, and Nancy Buchanan, dau. Theadore Buchanan—Nov. 22, 1809.

Riggle, Samuel, and Catherine Graybill (over 21)—May 3, 1796.

Riley, James, and Mary Fitsgerald—Feb. 7, 1791.

Rinehart, Abraham, and Catherine Niday. David Niday, surety—1795.

Rinhart, John, and Rosanna Custard, dau. John Custard—March 5, 1817.

Ripley, James H., and Polly Henry, dau. John Henry—March 1, 1815.

Ripley, William, and Betsy Murray, dau. Frederick Murray—May 19, 1820.

Risque, James, and Elizabeth Kimmerly—June 27, 1799.

Risque, James, and Rebecca Redd—July 4, 1799.

Roads, Mathias, and Martha Anderson, dau. William Anderson—March 13, 1810.

Roan, William, and Elizabeth Ellison—Jan. 27, 1778.

Roberts, James, and Ellinor Robers, dau. William—Jan. 25, 1795.

Roberts, Samuel, and Elizabeth Crush, dau. Peter Crush—July 18, 1807.

Robertson, Thomas, and Mary Day, widow of John—April 9, 1818.

Robinson, Edgar, and Hetty Wax, dau. Peter and Margarett Wax—Sept. 10, 1822.

Robinson, Edward, and Polly Anderson, dau. Joseph Anderson, dec.—Oct. 7, 1820.

Robinson, Henry, and Polly Darr, dau. Joseph Darr—Nov. 6, 1809.

Robinson, James, and Elizabeth Rogers, dau. John Rogers—June 19, 1805.

Robinson, John, and Mary Huggins—Nov. 25, 1799.

Robinson, John, and Polly Hoss, dau. Henry Hoss—Dec. 10, 1806.

Robinson, Samuel, and Margaret Smith, dau. Jacob Smith—Nov. 23, 1819.

Robinson, Simeon, and Catherine Painter, dau John Painter—March 24, 1820.

Robinson, Thomas, and Lusianna Brooks, dau. William Brooks—Jan. 2, 1810.

Robinson, William, and Mary Markspile, dau. Michael—Sept. 27, 1802.

Robinson, William, and Polly Franklin, dau. Lewis Franklin—June 25, 1807.

Rock, Andrew, and Merry McCroskey, dau. George—Sept. 9, 1818.

Rock, George, and Betsy McCoy, dau. Hugh McCoy, dec.—Oct. 13, 1811.

Rock, John, and Nancy C. McConnell—Oct. 19, 1820.

Rock, John, and Elizabeth Snodgrass—May 24, 1792.

Rock, Samuel, and Susanna Tate, dau. John Tate—April 15, 1818.

Rodehiffer, Samuel, and Mary Rinehart, dau. Francis Rinehart, dec.—Aug. 10, 1821.

Rodgers, George, and Catherine Styne, dau. Peter Styne—Feb. 7, 1805.

Rodgers, Joseph, and Mary Callender, dau.

Samuel Callender—Aug. 25, 1821.

Ronck-Ronk.

Ronck, Jacob, and Hannah Prother, dau. Thomas Prother—Dec. 20, 1803.

Ronk, John, and Catherine Markey—Dec. 3, 1800.

Ronk, Joseph, and Mary Showalter, dau. Henry—March 12, 1812.

Rose, Ezekiel, and Susanna Harmon, dau. George Harman—May 25, 1821.

Rose, James (son of William), and Anna Butcher, dau. Jacob—Aug. 17, 1814.

Rose, John, and Polly Hess (Hoss?)—Sept. 4, 1804.

Rose, John, and Mary McDonald—Dec. 11, 1777.

Rose, John, and Peggy Vogers, dau. Benjamin Vogers—Dec. 23, 1810.

Rose, William, and Rebecca Hamilton—April 25, 1799.

Rose, William, and Martha Persinger, dau. Jacob Persinger—Oct. 29, 1815.

Rowe, James, and Sophia Huffman—June 26, 1799.

Rowe, Stephen, and Barbary Huffman. John Huffman, surety—April 11, 1801.

Rowen, Charles, and Elizabeth Shaver. John Shaver, surety—Feb. 20, 1794.

Rowland, David, and Eliza Jordon, dau. John Jordon—June 3, 1811.

Rowland, James, and Sarah Kyle, dau. William Kyle—Jan. 25, 1802.

Rowland, William, and Nancy P. Luck, dau. John B. Luck—May 22, 1816.

Rowland, William, and Sarah Woods (over 21)—Oct. 3, 1819.

Royal, William, and Nnn Newport—Nov. 15, 1797.

Rucker, Clayburn, and Frances Ballard, dau. Elijah Ballard—Nov. 20, 1790.

Rud, John, and Elizabeth May, dau John May—May 27, 1809.

Rudeslle, Jacob, and Nancy Simpson—July 30, 1801.

Rule, Jacob, and Dolly Cox, dau. Christopher Cox—Dec. 14, 1803.

Rule, John, and Eve Copp, dau. Chris.—Dec. 31, 1818.

Rule, Michael, and Elizabeth Dill, dau. Henry Dill—Oct. 31, 1810.

Ruly, William, and Betsy Thompson, dau. Joseph Thompson—April 27, 1818.

Runnels, John, and Mary Baker, dau. George Baker—July 30, 1801.

Russell, Russel.

Russel, James, and Nancy Wufington. Consent by Jos. and Mary Wolkinson—Aug. 2,

1796.

Russall, John, and Anna Kimm, dau. George Kimm—Oct. 20, 1817.

Russel, John, and Mary Airs—Feb. 16, 1795.

Russel, Peter, and Sarah Wright, dau. Ann Arnold. Father dec.—Feb. 11, 1795.

Russell, William, and Nancy Wilson, dau. James Wilson—Feb. 22, 1817.

Rutter, Moses, and Catherine Wilson, dau. John Wilson—Feb. 23, 1790.

Rutteringer, Michael, and Elizabeth Refley, dau. David—Aug. 19, 1809.

—S—

Sadler, Jacob, and Mary Crowell, dau. Henry Crowell—Sept. 5, 1818.

Safely, Adam, and Melinda Ferrell, dau. Stephen Ferrell—July 22, 1819.

Sanmers, Henry, and Mary Horn, dau. Charles Horn—Nov. 29, 1805.

Sarber (Serber), Joseph, and Mary Stevens—Oct. 8, 1799.

Sarber, Henry, and Eleanor Flora—March 9, 1801

Sarver-Server.

Sarver, Alexander, and Elizabeth Miller, dau. Valentine Miller—Jan. 1, 1819.

Sarver, Casper, and Susanna Miller—Feb. 21, 1780.

Sarver, Henry, and Sarah Francisco, dau. Loderwick—Aug. 24, 1805.

Sarver, Isaac, and Frances Lake, dau. Israel Lake, dec.—March 19, 1810.

Sarver, James, and Catherine, Walker, dau. George Walker—Dec. 12, 1810.

Sarver, John, and Mary Smith—Jan. 10, 1797.

Sarver, Samuel, and Polly Tracy, dau. William Tracey, of Giles Co.—May 17, 1813.

Sarver, Samuel, and Mary Rowe. James Rowe, surety—Dec. 17, 1791.

Sawyers, John, and Rachel Rees. David Rees (her guardian), surety—March 8, 1791.

Sawyers, Thomas, and Margaret Rees. Consent by her mother, Margaret Rees—Jan. 3, 1797.

Scafford, Christley, and Elizazbeth Kesler (over 21), dau. George Kesler—Jan. 23, 1803.

Scantlin, James, Jr., son James, and Elizabeth Welch. Consent by Jane Welch, her guardian—1794.

Schroder, John George, and Marry Rennern—Dec. 20, 1781.

Scisson, Armstead, and Ann Hardy, dau. Thomas Hardy—Jan. 20, 1812.

Scott, Charles, and Polly Mahone, widow—June 9, 1812.

Scott, Henry, and Mary Price, dau. Thomas Price—Jan. 25, 1802.

Scott, Nathan, and Sarah Poague—Feb. 13, 1781.

Scott, Robert, and Susanna Urmy, dau. JacobUrmy—Dec. 15, 1814.

Scott, Sambrit, and Anna Mays, dau. Richard Mays—Feb. 9, 1787.

Scott, Samuel, and Rachel Sawyers, dau. Samsan and Agnes Sawyers—Feb. 12, 1785.

Scott, Samuel, and Sarah Baller—Sept. 14, 1790.

Scott, Samuel, and Caty Niday—ept. 1, 1798.

Scott, Samuel, and Frances Davis, dau. John, dec., and Catherine Davis—Aug. 9, 1816.

Scott, Zacheriah, and Mary Halfpain. John Halfpain, surety—March 20, 1795.

Seacat, Philip, and Elizabeth Stanback. Michael Stanback, surety—Dec. 26, 1800.

Seacrist, David, and Polly Floyd, dau. D. Floyd—March 30, 1814.

Seagle, Jacob, and Mary Way—April 9, 1795.

Sence, George, and Eve Catherine Young—March 16, 1812.

Sephyr, Hannon, and Mary Sawyer. Adam Sawyers,surety—May 12, 1798.

Sessler, Samuel, and Dorcas Brickey, dau. Peter Brickey—Jan. 15, 1822.

Sesson, James, and Polly Cartmill, dau. Henry Cartmill—Jan. 22, 1807.

Sexton, John, and Rebecca McDonald. Wm. Sexton, surety—Aug. 23, 1790.

Sexton, William, and Mary Ewing, dau. James Ewing—Aug. 3, 1790.

Shanklin, John, and Susannah Gilleland, dau. James Gilleland—Jan. 7, 1805.

Shanklin, Robert, and Polly Sharkey, dau. James Sharkey—May 18, 1802.

Shanklin, Samuel, and Mary Reyburn, dau. John Reyburn—July 14, 1789.

Shanklin, William, and Rachel Sharkey, dau. James Sharkey—Jan. 21, 1804.

Shanks, Adam, and Nancy Smiley, dau. Walter Smiley—April 22, 1817.

Shanks, Adam, and Betsy Frantz—Sept. 17, 1797.

Shanks, David, and Susan Johnston, dau. John Johnston—Jan. 11, 1820.

Shanks, Jacob, and Mary Rowland—April 13, 1819.

Shanks, Michael, and Sarah Rader, dau. Adam Rader—June 13, 1818.

Sharkey, Patrick, and Sally Allen, dau. John Allen—July 25, 1809.

Shartser, Benjamin, and Nancy White, dau. Peter White, dec.—Oct. 9, 1810.

Shartzer, Philip, and Mary Loyd, widow—June 8, 1813.

Shaver, Adam, and Hannah Harris. Thomas Harris, surety—Aug. 14, 1796.

Shaver, Adam, and Barbara Young, dau. Nicholas Young—Oct. 11, 1809.

Shaver, Andrew, and Susanna Bowers, dau. Jacob Bowers—Oct. 2, 1819.

Shaver, George, and Mary Glasper, dau. Richard Glasper—March 14, 1789.

Shaver, Jacob, and Judith Crapenter, dau. Joseph Carpenter—Aug. 9, 1786.

Shaver, Jacob, and Mary Rowland—April 13, 1819.

Shaver, Jacob, and Elizabeth Scott, dau. Joseph Scott—Sept. 7, 1793.

Shaver, John, and Margaret Wiley—June 15, 1800.

Shawver, George, and Elizabeth Karnes, dau. Jacob Karnes—Feb. 14, 1822.

Shawver, Samuel, and Jenny Shawver, dau. George Shawver—June 14, 1817.

Shepherd, Israel, and Agnes Enos (Knos?). Elija Knox, surety—Sept. 16, 1816.

Shepherd, William, and Elizabeth Beckner, dau. Joseph Beckner—March 23, 1819.

Sherman, Edmund, and Elizabeth Walton, dau. Wm. Walton—April 13, 1799.

Sherrad, James, and Mary Bumgardner, dau. Paulser Bumgardner—April 8, 1817.

Sherrad, Simon, and Catherine Hance. Consent by Grace Thompson—March 10, 1795.

Shetzer, Jacob, and Jane Hannah, dau. George Hannah, dec.—Jan. 5, 1815.

Shewey, Gasper, and Molly Beckner dau. Daniel Beckner—Aug. 17, 1805.

Shewey, Jacob, and Elizabeth Cook. Mathias Cok, surety—Feb. 16, 1820.

Shewey, Shue, and Matilda Alderson, dau. Thomas Alderson—Nov. 23, 1820.

Shewsberry, Benjamin, and Nancy Richardson, dau. William Richardson—Jan. 9, 1792.

Shields, John, and Anne Smith—July 31, 1786.

Shields, John, and Agnes Crow. James C. Crow. surety—Sept. 12, 1801.

Shields, Thomas, and Polly Moyers —Nov. 30, 1801.

Shields, William, and Mary Bryant. James Bryant, surety—April 2, 1801.

Shiff, John, and Ownie Deaton, dau. Elijah Deaton—Jan. 21, 1821.

Shipley, Robert, and Margarett Robinett. Consent by guardian, Jesse Robinett—March 17, 1788.

Shirkey, James, and Elizabeth Poague—Aug. 24, 1774.

Shirkey, John, and Jane Carroll—Jan. 12, 1780.

Shirkey, John, and Mary Thompson, dau.

John Thompson—Sept. 21, 1820.

Shirkey, Nicholas, and Sarah Woods, dau. Susanna and Michael Woods, of Montgomery County—Dec. 3, 1777.

Shirkey, Thomas, and Sarah Jefferson—Jan. 30, 1788.

Shoomaker, Leonard, and Unus Richey—April 11, 1787.

Shooman, Jacob, and Hannah Halderman, dau. Ch. and Elizabeth Halderman—March 10, 1804.

Short, David, and Jane Scott, dau. Nathan Scott—April 4, 1803.

Short, George, and Elizabeth Short—Feb. 2, 1819.

Short, Jessy, and Betsy Williamson, dau. John Williamson—Sept. 4, 1820.

Short, John, and Polly Harshbarger. Christian Harshbarger, surety—Oct. 19, 1799.

Short, John, and Eve Monical. Peter Monical, surety—March 27, 1800.

Short, John, and Sarah Hogan, dau. James Hogan—Dec. 17, 1815.

Shoup, Peter, and Margaret Huntsman—April 1, 1787.

Showalter, Abraham (son of Henry and under age), and Magdalene Ronck—March, 1812.

Showalter, Jacob (son Abraham), and Hannah Griffith—April 11, 1820.

Showalter, John (son, Samuel), and Mary Ronck, dau. George Ronck—Dec. 17, 1809.

Shull, John, and Rebecca Griffith. John Griffith, surety—May 28, 1800.

Shumate, George, and Polly Harmon, dau. William Harmon—Jan. 23, 1806.

Sifford, Adam, and Hannah Linkenhoger, dau. Elias Linkenhoger—Nov. 3, 1810.

Sifford, John, and Nancy Baker, dau. Samuel Baker—Dec. 13, 1801.

Silcock, Gabriel, and Sarah Hampton, dau. John Hampton—Feb. 17, 1793.

Silvers, Aaron, and Sally Wall, dau. Conrad Wall—Nov. 8, 1788.

Silvers, Aaron, and Sarah Sowder. Jacob Sowder, surety—Sept. 21, 1795.

Silvers, Jacob, and Jane Harkey—Jan. 31, 1793.

Simmons, Adam, and Sukey Crider, dau. Jacob. Christian Simmons, surety—April 24, 1792.

Simmons, Andrew ,and Rosanna Coon, dau. Michael Coon—Nov. 8, 1799.

Simmons, Christian, and Catherine Emmons. Ch. Emmons, surety—Aug. 8 1791.

Simmons, Ephriam, and Rutha Caldwell, dau. Hugh Caldwell—Aug. 1, 1805.

Simmons, Jonathan, and Polly Clapsaddle—Sept. 21, 1818.

Simmons, Philip, and Catherine Crater. Jacob Simmons, surety—March 26, 1788.

Simmons, Samuel, and Jane Chapman, dau. John Chapman—Aug. 18, 1812.

Simpson, Alexander, and Nancy Phillips. Richard Phillips, surety—June 13, 1800.

Simpson, John, and Hannah Evans, dau. William Evans—April 13, 1818.

Simpson, Solomon, and Mary Black—July 24, 1819.

Simpson, Solomon, and Elizabeth Lautern, dau. Reuben Lautern—March 21, 1793.

Sinclair, Wayman, and Elizabeth Douglas, dau. Benjamin Douglas—Feb. 17, 1793.

Sinoggin, Robert, and Narcissa Mills, dau. John Mills—June 29, 1797.

Sisson, Ludlow (son of Stanley), and Catherine Grissoe, dau. Matthew Grissoe—Jan. 25, 1817.

Sites, George, and Susanna Wysong, dau. Fiatt Wysong—Oct. 29, 1811.

Sites, John and Peggy Peck, dau. John Peck ,—March 28, 1809.

Sizer, Daniel, and Sarah Hardy, dau. Thomas Hardy— March 23, 1819.

Sizer, John, and Polly Crist, dau. Philip Crist—April 8, 1822.

Slater, Edward (of Frederick .Co), and Elizabeth Kean, dau. Samuel and Hannah Kean Oct. 18, 1788.

Slenker, William, and Nancy Brickey, dau. Peter Brickey—Oct. 3, 1810.

Sloan, David, and Catherine Statler, dau. Jacob Statler—Nov. 21, 1812.

Sloan, James, and Hannah Forrest, dau. Jamse Forrest, Jr.—Nov. 10, 1804.

Sligh, Jacob, and Sarah Silcock, widow of Gabriel—July 11, 1812.

Slow, John, and Mary Smith, dau. William Smith—Feb. 1, 1817.

Smalling, Thomas, and Cathy Kelley. Benj. Kelley, surety—Dec. 4, 1797.

Smiley, Alexander, and Susanna Ellison—May 24, 1782.

Smiley, Daniel, and Esther Richey, dau. Wm. Richey—June 23, 1789.

Smiley, Daniel, and Betsy Shank, dau. Christ. Shank—Sept. 4, 1809.

Smiley, George, and Mary Ellison. James Ellison, surety—April 30, 1787.

Smiley, James, and Betsy Knozworthy (his ward)—Sept. 14, 1819.

Smiley, James, and Martha Watkins, dau. Mary Watkins. Benj. Watkins, surety—Sept. 23, 1793.

Smiley, Walter, and Susan Krouse, dau. Jacob Krouse—May 1, 1821.

Smiley, William, Jr., and Ann Smiley. George Smiley, surety—May 23, 1785.

Smithers, Gabriel, and Jane McRoberts—May 19, 1772.

Smoot, John, and Barsy Henderson, dau. John Henderson, dec.—May 23, 1811.

Smith, Abraham, and Margaret Johnston. John Johnston, surety—Jan. 19, 1798.

Smith, Abraham, and Anne Gore. Michael Gore, surety—May 13, 1788.

Smith, Absolum, Jr., and Martha Garwood, dau. Joseph Garwood—Sept. 10, 1816.

Smith, Charles, and Prudence Dillon, dau. James Dillon, dec.—Oct. 2, 1819.

Smith, Elijah, and Susan Kessler, dau. David Kessler—May 8, 1820.

Smith, Harold, and Ann M. Bowyer, dau. Henry Bowyer—Nov. 21, 1816.

Smith, Henry, and Sally Shaver, dau. Abraham Shaver—Arpil 6, 1807.

Smith, Humphrey, and Elinor McCheny (of age). Cormack McCheny, suraty—July 1, 1785.

Smith, Isaac, and Mary Sevel—Aug. 12, 1783.

Smith, James, and Peggy Simmon, dau. William Simmon—Jan. 10, 1815.

Smith, John, and Rhody Pate. Jeremiah Pate (her bro.), surety—Feb. 14, 1801.

Smith, John, and Martha Wood—May 4, 1780.

Smith, John, and Mary Thomas, dau. James and Susannah. Abraham Smith, surety—Jan. 9, 1798.

Smith, Joseph, and Susannah Smith, dau. Jacob Smith—June 27, 1812.

Smith, Mishack, and Barbara Hammond—Nov. 1822.

Smith, Philip, and Polly Anderson—Feb. 3, 1820.

Smith, Rochard, and Patsy Ann Pitzer, dau. Barney Pitzer—Nov. 29, 1821.

Smith, Robert, and Hannah Preston. Terrance Conner, surety—Sept., 1787.

Smith, Robert, and Leah Kelly, dau. Thos. and Margaret Kelly. Alex Smith, surety—May 21, 1796.

Smith, Scott, and Matty McCafferty. Cormack McCafferty, ursety—Nov. 13, 1783.

Smith, Thomas, and Catherine Beckner, dau. Henry Beckner—Sept. 15, 1809.

Smith, William, and Polly Hoover, dau. Jacob Hoover—October 15, 1821.

Smith, William, and Susannah Bayne, dau. George Bayne—March 6, 1814.

Smyth, Benjamin, and Polly McDonald—8100.

Smyth, Henry, and Elizabeth Swain (Sovain?), dau. Abraham—Abraham—Oct. 10, 1797.

Smyth, John, and Betsy Watkins, dau. James Watkins—Sept. 12, 1809.

Smyth, Mathias, and Nancy Myers. Jacob Myers, surety—March 21, 1809.

Smyth, Michael, and Rebecca Hardy. Thomas Hardy, surety—Feb. 11, 1800.

Smyth, Peter, and Elizabeth Markley, dau. Nicholas Markley—Jan. 19, 1810.

Smyth, Thomas, and Nancy Crockett—Feb. 18, 1791.

Smyth, Thomas, and Mary Brough, dau. Daniel Brough—May 12, 1812.

Sneed, William, and Judith Haynins, dau. Benjamin—Oct. 9, 1820.

Snider, David, and Sarah Lemmon, dau. George Lemmon—April 9, 1810.

Snider, Henry, and Susannah Britz—March 24, 1800.

Snider, John, and Sarah Milling, dau. James Milling, dec.—Aug. 4, 1815.

Snider, John, and Hannah Noftzinger, dau. Peter Noftzinger—March 30, 1807.

Snider, John, and Lucy Dempsey, dau. Wm. Dempsey—Feb. 13, 1810.

Snider, Peter, and Mary Lemon, dau. George Lemon—Feb. 15, 1808.

Snyder, Philip, and Nancy Dolman, dau. Henry Dolman—Aug. 8, 1809.

Snodgrass, Alexander, and Elizabeth Smyth, dau. Jacob Smyth—Sept. 4, 1809.

Snodgrass, Henry, and Jesse Mann—Jan. 25, 1801.

Snodgrass, Isaac, and Jean Preston. Joseph Snodgrass, surety—May 1, 1800.

Snodgrass, James, and Elizabeth Fulton, dau. David Fulton. (Son of Joseph)—Sept. 26, 1790

Snodgrass, John, and Anne McClure, widow—March 14, 1817.

Snodgrass, Joseph (son Susy Snodgrass), and Susannah Snodgrass, dau. James and Margaret Snodgrass—July 10, 1787.

Snodgrass, Joseph, and Catherine Gish, dau. John Gish—March 20, 1804.

Snodgrass, Joseph (son of James), and Jannett Craddock, dau. Wm., dec.—Dec. 1, 1798.

Snodgrass, Robert, and Sarah Safley, dau. Henry Safley—Jan. 28, 1813.

Snodgrass, Robert, and Mary Walker, dau. John Walker—Nov. 3, 1819.

Snodgrass, William, and Esther Walker. Wm. Walker, surety—May 9, 1801.

Snodgrass, William, and Polly Nutter, dau. Zadok Nutter—Oct. 8, 1821.

Snow, William, and Margaret Vandine—Feb.

2, 1789.

Soff, Simon, and Sarah Crawford, dau. Patrick Crawford—Feb. 15, 1804.

Solenbarger, Joseph, and Susannah Stover—Jan. 3, 1799.

Souder, Jacob and Baddy Newgen—Jan. 10, 1787.

Souder, Jonathan, and Anne Nugent—Dec. 26, 1795.

Spalding, Ephriam, and Sarah Buttry—Dec. 19, 1797.

Specklemoyer, Samuel, and Susannah Thompson, dau. James Thompson—Sept. 18, 1787.

Sperry, David, and Catherine Gish, dau. Jacob Gish—July 25, 1819.

Spessard, John, and Susannah Peters, dau. Jacob Peters—Feb. 17, 1817.

Spicard, Philip, and Catherine Sovain. Abraham Sovain, surety—Feb. 28, 1793.

Spigle, Michael, and Martha Grifl, dau. John Grill, dec.—May 4, 1818.

Sproul, Alexander, and Elizabeth Right, dau. eter Right. John Sproul, surety—March 16, 1792.

Spurlock, David, and Hannah Flower. Consent by Thomas and Prudence Flower, "as he is a good young man"—Jan. 17, 1786.

Spyker, David, and Batsy McCarroll, dau. James McCarroll, of Tenn.—Dec. 9, 1811.

Squires, Levi, and Milly Banks, dau. John Banks—Sept. 3, 1803.

Stair, Henry, and Salofy Brough, dau. Daniel Brough—June 13, 1819.

Stair, Jacob, and Susanna Flook, dau. Peter Flook—Jan. 1, 1821.

Starr, John, and Elizabeth Lanius, dau. Jacob Lanius—Sept. 22, 1814.

Starry, John, and Elizabeth Harshbarger, dau. Christian Harshbarger—March 21, 1815.

Stayley-Staley.

Stayley, Andrew, and Nancy Brown, dau. Hugh Brown, dec.—June 27, 1803.

Staley, Jacob, and Drucilla McCoy, dau. Thomas McCoy—Oct. 7, 1804.

Staley, Malcher, and Sarah Camper, dau. John Camper—Oct. 20, 1815.

Staley, Malichi, and Mary Wallace, dau. James Wallace—April 18, 1820.

Staley, Peter, Jr., and Hannah Level—Sept. 27, 1809.

Staley, Stephen, and Betsy Deardorf, dau. Heanry Deardorf—Oct. 3, 1809.

Stanback, David, and Mary Kelly, dau. John Kelly—Dec. 7, 1810.

Stanback, Jesse, and Elizabeth Kelly, dau.

John Kelly, Sr.—Feb. 20, 1812.

Starkey, John, and Jane George—Jan. 12, 1780.

Starrett, Robert, and Sally Brooks, dau. James Brooks—Nov. 12, 1805.

Statler, Abraham, and Catherine Beckner—March 21, 1801.

Statler, Abraham, and Magdalena Seacat, dau. Charles Seacat—Dec. 8, 1817.

Statler, Abraham, and Hannah Miller, widow of David Miller—Dec. 18, 1810.

St. Clair, Christian, and Elizabeth Painter, dau. Henry Painter—Oct. 27, 1822.

St. Clair, George, and Betsy Snodgrass, dau. Joseph Snodgrass—Sept. 14, 1805.

Steel, Andrew, and Margaret McFerran, dau. Samuel McFerran—Mrach 3, 1789.

Steel Robert, and Elizabeth Wilson, dau. Mary and Matthew, latter dec.—Sept. 13, 1803.

Steel, Samuel, and Betsy S. Taylor, dau. James Taylor, dec. No date on bond in 1818.

Steel, William, and Jane Bayne, dau. George Bayne—Dec. 19, 1814.

Steenson, John, and Phebe Glendy, dau. James Glendy—Dec. 11, 1783.

Steinberger, Peter, and Mariah Jordon, dau. John Jordon, "esquire"—Nov. 30, 1807.

Steinberger, William, and Elizabeth Beale—July 20, 1797.

Stepp, George, and Sidney Mills, dau. John Mills—June 27, 1803.

Sterling, Henry (son of Samuel), and Elinor Sterling, dau. John Sterling—Jan. 25, 1790.

Stevens, Jacob, and Sally Hartman, dau. George Hartman—March 13, 1811.

Stevens, John, and Elizabeth Hudson—Jan. 31, 1782.

Stevens, Michael C., and Mary Seagle—Dec. 13, 1819.

Stevens, Solomon, and Milly Britt—May 26, 1781.

Stever - see Stiver.

Stewart - see Stuart.

Stewart, James, James, and Elizabeth Bush, dau. Peter Bush—March 1822.

Stewart, John, and Mary Neiswanger, dau. Jacob Nieswanger—Feb. 8, 1796.

Stewart, William, and Catherine Vineyard, dau. Christian Vineyard, dec.—Nov. 24, 1816.

Stewart, William, and Amey Reynolds, dau. Silas Reynolds—Feb. 1, 1786.

Stiver, Henry, and Catherine Thrasher, dau. Christopher Thrasher—Feb. 22, 1803.

Stiver, Isaac, and Catherine Burbaker, dau. Adam Brubaker—May 30, 1815.

Stone, William, and Jane Wilson, dau. John Wilson, dec.—Dec. 19, 1820.

Stoner, Jacob, and Barbara Gharst, dau. Abraham Gharst—Feb. 12, 1821.

Stoner, John, and Polly Hamilton, dau. Andrew Hamilton—Feb. 23, 1810.

Stoner, John, and Elizabeth Gish, dau. David Gish—March 3, 1817.

Stover, Abraham, and Amy Rader, dau. Adam Rader—June 29, 1811.

Stover, Daniel, and Polly Frantz, dau. Michael Frantz—April 8, 1806.

Stover, George, and Anna Rader, dau. Adam Rader—Nov. 1, 1810.

Stover, Jacob, and Susannah Solonbarger. Wm. Stover, surety—March 19, 1798.

Stover, John, and Caty Snider. Henry Snider, surety—Oct. 28, 1801.

Stover, John, and Sally Coon, dau. Jacob Coon—Oct. 9, 1819.

Stover, Michael, and Elizabeth Solenbarger—Feb. 4 1799.

Strough, George Michael, and Ol Minter, dau. Christopher Minter—May 1, 1805.

Stuart - see Stewart.

Stuart, John, and Ruthy Reed, dau. Wm. and Ruth Reed—Feb. 14, 1789.

Stuart, Robert, and Polly Green, dau. James Green—Nov. 7, 1805.

Stuart, Robert, and Elizabeth Rowland, dau. Thomas Rowland—Feb. 20, 1810.

Stull, Daniel and Sarah Patterson—May 6, 1799.

Stull, George, and Jane Bep (Bass), dau. Christopher—July 16, 1806.

Stull, John, and Mary Wood, dau. Joseph Wood—March 31, 1804.

Suber, Joseph, and Mary Stevens—Nov. 8, 1799.

Sucrest, John, and Rosanna Daun—April 28, 1787 (see Secrist).

Sullenbarger, Michael, and Betsy Himer, dau. John Himer, dec—April 27, 1809.

Summerfield, Absolum, and Catherine Smith, dau. Jacob Smith—Dec. 29, 1813.

Summerfield, Benjamin, and Polly Mean, dau. Hugh Mean—Dec. 12, 1822.

Summerfield, James, and Polly Caldwell, dau. John Caldwell—Nov. 12, 1821.

Summerfield, Samuel, and Fanny Lewis Parrish. Julius Summerfield, surety—Sept. 3, 1798.

Summerfield, William, and Catherine Maggett, dau. Absolum Maggett—Aug. 2, 1792.

Summers, Henry, and Mary Horn, dau. Charles Horn—Nov. 29, 1805.

Summers, John, and Elizabeth Myers, dau.

Samuel Myers—May 13, 1822.

Surber, Jacob, and Nancy Waggoner, widow of John—Feb. 10, 1819.

Sutherland, Henry, and Agnes Leforce, dau. Samuel Leforce—Jan. 8, 1806.

Sutton, John, and Winny Runnion—Sept. 4, 1783.

Swainey, Terrance, and Elizabeth Minnick—March 5, 1795.

Sweetland, Eleazer, and Sally Vanmeter—Dec. 20, 1814.

Switzer, James, and Mary Higgins, dau. Peter Higgins, dec.—May 13, 1815.

Switzer, John and Rosanna Caldwell, dau. Robert Caldwell, dec. Her mother, Mary—Nov. 15, 1790.

Switzer, John, and Elizabeth Lockhart. Nathan Switzer, surety—Aug. 9, 1800.

Switzer, Joseph (under age), and Catherine Moomaw, lau. Christopher, dec.—March 24, 1812.

Switzer, Madison Monroe, and Lucy Ann Linkenhoger, dau. George Linkenhoger—Oct. 5, 1831.

Switzer, Nathan, and Elizabeth Chenowith, —Jan. 11, 1791.

Switzer, Robert, and Susanna Robinson, dau. John Robinson—March 20, 1819.

Switzer, Robert C., and Letitia C. Doss, dau. John Doss—March 20, 1819.

Switzer, Thomas, and Mary Young—May 26, 1819.

Switzer, William, and Ann Bridger. Wm. Dougherty, surety—March 9, 1787.

Switzer, William, and Abagail Darr, dau. Joseph Darr—Aug. 24, 1809.

—T—

Tagoe, Abraham, and Susannah Short—Feb. 12, 1800.

Talbot, Williston, and Esther Carper. Jacob Carper, surety—Jan. 5, 1795.

Tapscott, (aged 21) James, and Margaret Katon—1803.

Tate, David, and Comfort Knox, dau. Elisha Knox—Aug. 11, 1784.

Tate, Edward, and Sarah McMullin, dau. Edward McMullin—July 8, 1786.

Tate, James, and Mary Loyd, dau. Thomas Loyd—Feb. 17, 1783.

Tate, James, and Charlotte Beale, widow of Madison Beale—Jan. 20, 1819.

Tathern, John, and Mary Adkins, "relic of John L. Adkins"—Dec. 6, 1796.

Taylor, David, and Ann Hannah, dau. Alexander Hannah—April 16, 1809.

Taylor, Frederick, and Magg Florian. George

Florian, surety—Dec. 20, 1797.

Taylor, Isaac, and Elizabeth Street, dau. Wm. Street—Nov. 25, 1785.

Taylor, Isaac, and Susanna Smith—Jan. 9, 1786.

Taylor, James, and Ann Tillery. John Tillery, surety—Jan. 5, 1778.

Taylor, James, and Rebecca McDonald. Walter McDonald, surety—Jan. 22, 1785.

Taylor, John, and Mary Maggett, dau. John Maggett—Oct. 15, 1804.

Taylor, John, and Sarah Brammer, dau. John Brammer—Feb. 2, 1821.

Taylor, Jonathan, and Mary Kelly—Aug. 5, 1777.

Taylor, Joseph L., and Hannah Reynolds, dau. John Reynolds—June 4, 1801.

Taylor, Thomas, and Elizabeth Boyl, dau. Wm. Boyl—Aug. 5, 1794.

Taylor, William, and Margaret Tummons—Feb. 31, 1781.

Templeton, Ezekiel, and Elizabeth Hartman, dau. George Hartman—Nov. 1, 1815.

Tennison, Ezekiel, and Jane Stratton, dau. John Stratton—Sept. 14, 1819.

Terry, John, and Esther Brown. Thomas Brown, surety—bF .e2, 1781.

Terry, Miles, and Hannah Horton—Jan. 30, 1782.

Terry, Stephen, and Alice Biggs, dau. Edward Biggs—Nov. 21, 1792.

Thomas, Elias, and Mary Spessard, dau. Michael Spessard—Sept. 29, 1821.

Thomas, Jonathan, and Hannah Potts—July 3, 1786.

Thomas, Lewis, and Polly Buser, dau. Frederick Buser—Mya 7, 1816.

Thomason, John, and Elizabeth Garwood, dau. Joseph Gardoow—Dec. 15, 1808.

Thomason, Preston, and Elizabeth Staley, dau. Abraham Staley—May 5, 1816.

Thomison, John, and Nancy Preston, dau. John Preston—Nov. 23, 1809.

Thompson, Creed, and Eliza F. Coleman, dau. Eleazer Coleman—Jan. 10, 1821.

Thompson, Henry, and Polly Crush, dau. Henry Crush—Jan. 25, 1810.

Thompson, James, and Mary Scott, dau Nathan Scott—Dec. 16, 1817.

Thompson, James, and Mary Brown, dau. Thomas Brown—April 12, 1813.

Thompson, John, and Winifred Brickey. Jarrett Brickey, surety—June 21, 1781.

Thompson, John, and Anna Walton, dau. William Walton—March 23, 1811.

Thompson, Joshua, and .... Gantsby—Dec. 12, 1786.

Thompson, Nelson, and Delinda Feazel, dau. Philip Feazel—Aug. 30, 1822.

Thompson, Thomas, and Anne McNeal—June 17, 1784.

Tipton, Joshua, and Jannett Shields. Thomas Shields, surety—Aug. 16, 1785.

Titus, Joseph and Elizabeth Matthews—May 6 1775.

Tolbert, John, and Elizabeth Foster. James M, Early, surety—Aug. 30, 1790.

Tosh, James, and Anne Broadwater— May 11, 1787.

Towles, Oliver, and Agatha Lewis, dau. William—Dec. 28, 1798.

Townley, John, and Christina Markey, dau. Nicholas Markey. Feb., 25, 1811

Townley, Robert, and Rebecca Eddrick, Dec. 3, 1799.   ,

Traclor, Henry and Elizabeth Helmontoler. Michael Helmontoler, surety. Oct. 3, 1796.

Treamor, George, and Sarah Garwood, dau. Joseph Garwood. Nov. 8, 1810.

Trent, John, and Elizabeth Lewis, William Lewis, surety Sept., 28, 1795.

Tressler, John, and Mary Fudge, dau. Christian Fudge. Nov. 8 1810.

Tressler, William and Margaret Brummer, dau. John Brummer. May 26, 1820.

Trigg, Stephen, and Polly Harvey. Robert Harvey, surety. June 18, 1795.

Trigg, William, and Susannah Smith, dau. Francis Smith. Aug., 18, 1795.

Tucker, Armistead, and Patience Franklin, dau. Francis. Dec. 31, 1816.

Turk, Samuel, and Mary Moody. Sept. 24 1796.

Turman, Charles, and Lucy Hilton, dau. Elijah and Susannah Hilton. Nov. 14, 1786.

Turman, Samuel and Barbara Shauman. Oct. 23, 1786.

Turner, Adam and Delilah Turner, dau. William Turner. Sept., 15, 1809.

Turner, Ezekiah, and Sarah Hornel (aged 21), dau. William Hornel. 1803.

Turner, Gilbreath, and Eleanor Terry, widow of Stephen Terry. May 13, 1810.

—U—

Urmy, Abraham, and Anna Frantz, dau. Michael Frantz. Jan., 18, 1809.

—V—

Vandergrift, John, and Barbara Wiseman, dau. Frederick Wisemtn. Sept. 12, 1812.

Vanmeter, Joseph, and Damaris Lockland, dau. Elisha Lockland. Sept., 7, 1815.

Vansant, Vansandt.

Vansant, Elisha, and Elinor Willson, James Willson, surety. Aug. 1, 1784.

Vansant, Elisha, and Margaret Crawford, dau. Andrew Crawford. April 8, 1788.

Vansant, Isiah, and Margaret Thompson, Aug., 11, 1782.

Vansant Isiah, and Elinor Willson, dau. James Willson. Oct. 10, 1821.

Vanover, Henry (son, Cornelius) and Martha Bandy. dau. Richard Bandy. June7, 1794.

Vaughn, James, and Margaret Wort, dau. Andrew Wort. Feb. 7, 1815.

Veal, David, and Susanna Peterman, dau. Jacob Peterman. March 30, 1809.

Veal, Thomas, tand Mary Keer. March 11, 1782.

Vineyard, Christian, and Elizabeth Gish, dau. Jacob Gish. Feb. 15, 1817.

Vineyard, Christian, and Elizabeth Britz, dau. Adam Britz. May 14, 1798.

Vineyard Nicholas, and Margaret Thraver, dau. Frederick Thrasher. Nov., 25, 1816.

Vineyard, William, and Rebecca Horn, dau. Charles Horn. Dec. 16 1811.

W ....

Waddle David, and Keiah Dehart, Jan. 10, 1786.

Wagg, William, and Sarah Martin, dau. George Martin. June 16, 1804.

Waggoner, Jacob, and Margaret Britz, dau. Adam Britz, May 31 1807.

Waggoner John, and Mary Powers, dau. Yancy Powers, Dec. 14, 1816.

Walden, Moses, and Mary St. Clair. March 5, 1804.

Wales, Martin, and Nancy Buford, dau. William Buford. Jan. 3, 1791.

Walker Daniel, and Catherine Myers, dau. Henry Myers. April 8, 1816.

Walker, Frederick, and Elizabeth Hendrickson, dau. Zacheriah Hendrickson, Oct. 24, 1812.

Walker, George, and Elinder Looney, dau. John Looney, Sr. Dec. 18 1805.

Walker, Henry, and Martha Woods, Andrew Woods surety. Dec. 27, 1781.

Walker James, and Margaret Woods, Andrew Woods, surety. March 2, 1772.

Walker James, and Jane Carden, dau. Joseph Carden. Sept. 10, 1803.

Walker, Jesse, and Susanna Clagg, dau. Alexander Clagg. Dec. 24 1799.

Walker, John, and Esther Looney, George Walker, surety. June 15, 1802.

Walker, Oliver, and Million Webb, dau. Julius Webb. June 8, 1779.   z   z   z

Walker, Peter, and Polly Englehart, Feb. 15, 1820.

Walker, Reuben, and Elizabeth Jamison, widow John, and dau. John Douglas. June 12, 1815.

Walker, Robert, and Jane Allen, dau. Moses Allen. Jan. 8, 1811.

Walker, Robert, and Sophia Biggs, dau. John Biggs. Dc. 2, 1805.

Walker, Samuel, and Susanna McDonald, Oct. 26, 1786.

Walker, Thomas, anl Sally Patzell. Dec. 21, 1818.

Walker, William, and Elinor Moore (21 "next Sept.") dau. Joseph Moore, of Ky. May 29, 1806.

Walker, William, and Mary Walker, April 25, 1786.

Wall, Adam, and Mary Ann Matthews. March 1, 1797.

Wall, John, and Dorcus Mattox, Scholfield Mattox, surety. Consent by Conrad Wall, Dec. 22 1792.

Wallace, Caleb, and Rosanna Christian. Joseph Christian, surety. May 10, 1779.

Wallace, James, and Dolly Bogan. March 8, 1797.

Wallace, Robert, and Anne Cartmill, dau. James Cartmill. Wm. Wallace, surety, Dec. 10, 1789.

Wallace, Samuel, and Rebecca Bilbro, dau. Wm. Bilbro. Feb. 22, 1806.

Walters, John, and Susanna Givens, dau. Daniel Givens. Oct. 7, 1791.

Ward, Flan, and Elizabeth Dennis, dau. Joseph and Mary Dennis. Sept. 1 1792.

Ward, Joshua, and Rhoday Stiff. July 8, 1794.

Warner, Aaron and Susanna Simmons. April 6, 1810.

Watkins, John and Catherine Lemon, dau. Peter Lemon. April 4, 1817.

Watkins, John, and Mary Lindsey, Walter Lindsey surety. July 30, 1794.

Watkins, John, and Milard Jones, dau. Ambrose Jones. Jan. 28, 1804.

Watkins, Moses, and Nancy Jones, Allen Jones, surety. Jan. 14, 1800.

Watkins, Moses, and Anna Baird, dau. Thomas Baird. Feb. 24, 1817.

Watterson, Joseph, (son Capt. Henry), and Ann McGeorge, dau. Thomas McGeorge. Sept. 9, 1807.

Watterson, William, and Agnes Shanklin, dau. Robert and Rebecca Shanklin. Oct. 22 1788.

Watts, Edward, and Elizabeth Breckenridge, dau. Gen. James Breckenridge. May 6, 1811.

Wattwood, George, and Margaret Franklin. Jan. 27, 1779.

Wayman, Henry, and Margaret Francis, dau. Joseph and Betsy Francis, father, dec. Nov. 1, 1813.

Wax, Henry, and Catherine Book, dau. Michael Book. Oct. 19 1803.

Wears, see Weirs.

Wears, Philip, and Ann Voltain, dau. John Voltain. July 2, 1782.

Webb, George, and Nancy Knuckles. John Knuckles surety. Feb. 13, 1795.

Webb, James, and Jane Claxton. Nov. 30 1784.

Webb, Josiah, and Margaret Crow dau. William Crow. Nov. 9, 1790.

Webb, Julius, and Ann Givens dau. Dab. Givens. Dec. 13, 1790.

Webster, (son, Samuel), and Elizabeth Reynolds. dau. Joseph Reynolds. Nov. 9, 1807.

Weddle, William, and Mary Gilkerson. Jan. 7 1799.

Weirs, James, and Elizabeth Shirkey, dau. James Shirkey dec. Sept. 20 1810.

Weirs, Joseph, and Hannah McCreary, widow of John. March 5 1806.

Weirs, William, and Betsy Caldwell, dau. George Caldwell. Dec. 22, 1804.

Weist, Peter, and Mary Smith. Wm. Smith, surety. Sept. 12, 1788.

Welch, Benjamin, and Charlotte Pitzer. Jan. 28, 1817.

Welch, Daniel, and Elizabeth Ward, dau. John Ward, dec. July 7, 1804.

Welch John, and Esther Thing, dau. William and Mary Thing. May 23, 1789.

Welch, Stephen, and Polly Stanford Davis, dau. William. Oct. 17, 1809.

Welch, William, and Mary Young, dau. Jacob Young, March 23, 1821.

Wertz Peter, and Elizabeth Shaver, dau. Andrew Shaver, dec. Sept. 21, 1820.

West, Tilghman, and Polly Mitchell, dau. Rev. Edward Mitchell. April 4, 1803.

West, Capt. Washington, and Frances Mitchell, dau. Rev. Edward Mitchell. April 23, 1811.

Wheat, Reason, and Soloma Cole, dau. John Cole. Dec. 27, 1824.

Wheeless, John, and Susannah Icenburger, dau. Paul Icenbburger. March 20, 1805.

White, Benjamin, and Fanny Lavender, dau. Robert Lavender. June 1, 1811.

White, Edmund P., and Sarah McClanahan, dau. Elijah McClanahan. Oct. 4, 1824.

White, John, and Agnes Martin, Dec. 20, 1796.

White, John, and Jane Caldwell, dau. Ro. Caldwell, dec. May 26, 1821.

White Jonathan, and Polly Hampton. John Hampton, surety. June 22, 1796.

White, Samuel, and Sarah Handiford, Aug. 15, 1787.

Whitehead, William, and Margaret Hutcheson, Jan. 25, 1785.

Whitley, Jonathan, and Sarah Cunningham, dau. Rebeckah Cunningham. Aug. 11, 1773.

Whitmore, John, and Catherine Sheets, dau. John Sheets. April 22, 1809.

Whitner, Jacob, and Caty Short, Sept. 1, 1800.

Whitten Lewis, and Charlotte Goodwin, dau. James Goodwin. April 6, 1818.

Wiat, Henry, and Polly Lavender, dau. Thomas Lavender. Oct. 14, 1819.

Wickham, John, and Rebeckah Dodd. Consent by Susannah Barton, Wm. Dodd, surety. 1785.

Wilhelm, Isaac, and Susanna Owen. March 2, 1807.

Wilhelm, Peter, and Caty Harshbarger, Christian Harshbarger, surety—March 23, 1801.

Wilkinson, William, and Sarah Piatt, dau. Benjamin Piatt. Dec. 25, 1804.

Willcocks, Benjamin, and Mary Kelly. Sept. 24, 1787.

Willes, Hugh, and Sarah Allbright, dau. George Allbright, dec. Sept. 12, 1809.

Willfong, (Wilsong?) Jacob, and Nary McCorkle, dau. Patrick McCorkle. Feb. 3, 1786.

Williams, John, and Elizabeth Rock, dau. John Rock, Sept. 9, 1807.

Williams Philip, anl Jane Polk, dau. Joseph Polk Sr. May 8, 1804.

Williams, Thomas, and Rachel Casteel, James Casteel, surety. April 20, 1779.

Williams William, andMargaret Bryan, dau. James Bryan. March 7, 1814.

Williams, William, and Rachel Falls, dau. John Falls. Oct. 12, 1801.

Williams, William, and Margaret McCarroll, dau. Jamec McCarroll. Sept. 14. 1802.

Williamson, Vlement, (son, John) and Polly Farmer, dau. Conrad Farmer. Oct. 16, 1804.

Williamson, Henry, and Isabella Armstrong. Robert Armstrong, surety. Nov. 30, 1795.

Williamson, James, and Nancy McCorkle. Patrick McCorkle, surety. Sept. 30, 1788.

Wills, James, and Lucy Gaunt. Oct. 16, 1794.

Willmore, Thomas, anl Judith Dempsey dau. William Dempsey, dec. June 11, 1806.

Wilson - Willson

Wilson, Alexander, and Rebekah Gillespie. Simon Gillespie, surety. June 10, 1798.

Wilson, Bryden, (son, Thomas) and Sarah Galbreath dau. Thomas Galbreath. Feb.

22, 1809.

Wilson, George, and Jean Wallen. James Wilson, surety. Nov. 9, 1784.

Wilson, James, and Mary Hackett, dau. Thomas Hackett. June 23, 1798.

Wilson, James, and Elizabeth McClure, Sept. 5. 1785.

Wilson, James, and Nancy Platt, dau. Benjamin Platt—Dec. 25, 1804.

Wilson, James, and Nancy Harrison, dau. James Harrison. Nov. 27, 1809.

Wilson, John, and Eliza Gilliford, dau. Allen Gilliford. March 18, 1804.

Wilson, John, and Mary Moore. James Moore, surety. May 28, 1800.

Wilson, John, and Rosanna Dennis, dau. Joseph Dennis. Jan. 7, 1790.

Wilson, John, and Tibatha S. Doss, widow of Jesse. March 2, 1819.

Wilson, Josiah, and Sarah Crawford dau. John Crawford. Oct. 22 1818.

Wilson Nathaniel, and Elinor Edmundson. June 11, 1797.

Wilson, Richard, and Margaret Fulton, Nov. 30, 1784.

Wilson Robert, and Jenny McNeel. June 16, 1806.

Wilson, Robert, and Jane Summerfield, dau. Richard and Sarah. Jan. 19, 1795.

Wilson, Samuel, and Pricilla Fleming, dau. Col. Wm. Fleming, dec. Feb. 15 1806.

Wilson, Thomas, and Elizabeth McDonald, dau. Daniel McDonald, Nov. 17, 1809.

Wilson Thomas, and Mary Edmundson. June 11, 1797.

Wilson, Thomas, and Esther Walker, dau. Wm. Walker—Oct. 28, 1791.

Win, Joseph, an dHannah McCreary, widow John McCreary. April 5, 1806.

Winard, Adam, and Elizabeth Baker, dau. Robert Baker. March 27, 1806.

Windard, Jacob, and Barbara Bowers, Feb. 2 1797.

Wingart, Henry, and Magdalene Frantz, dau. Michael Frantz. Oct. 5, 1822

Wingart Martin, and Elizaebth Frantz, dau. Michael Frantz, March 14, 1818.

Wiseman, Richard, and Polly Hort, dau. George Hart. Oct. 21, 1822.

Wisler John, and Anna Spiller, dau. Jacob Spiller. April 4, 1820.

Witcher John, and Margaret May, dau. John May. July 18, 1822.

Withrow, William, and Mary Snodgrass, dau. Isaac Snodgrass. Sept. 2, 1802.

Wittington, Thomas, and Alice Brady. Dec. 2, 1779.

Wolf, James, (son of Michael) and Susannah Little, dau. William Little. Dec. 8, 1802.

Wolf, Peter, and Catherine Calor, dau. John Calor. July 26 1803.

Woltz, Abraham, and Margaret Caldwell, dau. Hugh Caldwell. June 3, 1813.

Woltz, Ceorge, and Hetty Anderson. Jan. 30, 1800.

Woltz, John, and Peggy Woland, dau. Jacob Woland. June 24, 1806.

Woltz, Jacob, and Nancy Brilgeland, George Woltz surety. Feb. 27, 1802.

Womack William, anl Jane Poage, widow of John Poage. Nov. 1, 1810.

Woodard, George and Charlotte Mourn. May 10, 1794.

Wood, Adam, and Ann Shirkey. May 27, 1772.

Wood, James and Sarah Shephers dua. Dubartes Shepherd, Oct. 20, 1806.

Wood James, and Elizabeth Shewsberry dau. Dabney Shewsberry, dec. Feb. 12, 1821.

Wood James, and Peggy Brookman dau. John Brookman. Nov. 28 1813.

Wood, James L., and Sally Lewis, dau. Andrew Lewis dec. Aug. 2 1815.

Wood William, and Peggy Williamson, dau. John Williamson. May 22, 1819.

Woods David, and Elizabeth Fulwiler, dau. Jacob Fulwiler. Oct. 14, 1817.

Woods, Edward, and Sally Gilleland, dua. James Gilleland. Sept. 24 1805.

Woods, Edward (son of Samuel), and Anna Shepherd (over 21) dau. Dobartes Shepherd, Oct. 29, 1802.

Woods, Enos, and Mary Kelly—Oct. 19, 1799.

Woods John, and Elizabeth Smith. Absolun Smith, surety. March 24, 1797.

Woods, Joseph and Isabella Eakin. Oct. 26, 1798.

Woods, Richard, (son of Samuel) and Rebecca Wilson. Alex Wilson, surety. April 12 1796.

Woods, Samuel (mother, Eliabeth), and Jane Green, dau. Edward Green—July 17, 1778.

Woods, Samuel and Henrietta Kelley, dau. Mary Kelley—Sept. 10, 1802.

Woodruff, Adrion, and Nancy Russell—May 14, 1799.

Woolwine, Jacob, and Mary Bailor, over 21—April, 11, 1802.

Woodley, Michael, and Jane Mann. Jno. Gillespie, surety—Aug. 13, 1779.

Worder, Robert, and Nancy Walker, dau. John Walker—Nov. 25, 1793.

Worth, Evan, and Durzella Beane, dau Josiah Beane—June 10, 1814.

Worts, John, and Anne Frantz—March 21, 1812.

Worts, John, and Sarah Henry, dau. Wm. Henry—May 24, 1815.

Worts, Samuel, and Margaret McEhenny, dau. Samuel McEhenny—Sept. 16, 1814.

Worts, William, and Elizabeth Bowers. Martin Bowres, surety—Sept. 26, 1795.

Wray, David, and Elizabeth Carvin—Feb. 11, 1797.

Wright, Charles, and Eunice Caldwell, dau. Hugh Caldwell—Sept. 9, 1816.

Wright, Charles, and Nancy Mann—Sept. 22, 1794.

Wright, Jacob, and Agnes McMillen. Wm. McMillen, surety—April 15, 1799.

Wright, James, and Elizabeth Black, dau. James Black—April 3, 1781.

Wright, John (son of John), and Jane Andrews—Nov. 16, 1815.

Wright, John, and Catherin Persinger. Jno. Persinger, surety—Oct. 12, 1785.

Wright, John, and Anne Coher—Sept. 8, 1778.

Wright, John and Agnes McMurray, dau. William MccMcurray—Aug. 13, 1789.

Wright, Peter, and Sally Persinger, dau. Jacob Persinger, Sr.—Dec. 27, 1812.

Wright, Peter, and Mamcy Cook, over 21—May 16, 1797.

Wright, Richard, and Catherine Dame, dau. George Dame—April 25, 1805.

Wright, William, and Rachel Sawyers, dau. Solomon and Agnes Sawyers—Feb. 13, 1789.

Wrightsman, Daniel, and Catherine, Bolton, dau. Henry Bolton—March 7, 1815.

Wrightsman, John, and Chrsitina Coulter—Aug. 10, 1784.

Wrightsman, John, Jr. (under age and son of John), and Susanna Kinzey, dau. Christian—July 11, 1805.

Wrightsman, Samuel, and Anne Houtz, dau. Leonard Houtz—June 9, 1812.

Writter, Daniel, and Barbara Himes, dau. John Himes—Jan. 18, 1803.

Wyand, Jacob, and Elizabeth Riddlebarger, dau. John Riddlebarger—Nov. 6, 1811.

Wysong, Fyette, and Susanna Coffman, dau. Henry Coffman—May 27, 1814.

Wysong, Joseph, and Mary Smtih. Isaac Smtih, surety—July 7, 1798.

—Y—

Yates, Jonathan, and Nancy Sutherland. James Sutherland, surety—June 10, 1800.

Yeargin, John, and Elizabeth Tate, widow of Nathaniel G. Tate—Oct. 24, 1812.

Yoakum, George, and Esabella Taylor—Oct.

5, 1780.

Yopp, William, and Siby Litton. Father dec. —Sept. 24, 1807.

Yost, Henry, and Polly Early, dau. James Matten Early—Aug. 17, 1805.

Young, Daniel, and Elizabeth Capp, dau. Christopher Capp—Feb. 11, 1809.

Young, Henry, and Rebecca Fender, dau. Frederick Fender—Aug. 27, 1814.

—Z—

Zeagler, John, and Elizabeth Heck, dau.

Peter Heck—Aug. 24, 1813.

Zell, Peter, and Catherine Graybill, dau. Daniel Graybill—Oct. 25, 1818.

Zell, Thomas, and Patsy Pogue—July 24, 1819.

Zimmerman, George, and Susanna Kessler, dau. John Kessler—Dec. 20, 1819.

Zimmerman, Jacob, and Nancy Cartman, dau. eter Cartman—June 19, 1820.

Zoll, Jacob, and Nancy Brough, dau. John Brough—Jan. 26, 1804.

Zurkle, Peter, and Mary Glasburn, dau. David Glasburn—Nov. 8, 1810.

Wills and Deeds of Botetourt County

—A—

Aikins, Redmon, Pro. Nov. 1781, a non-cupative will. Names children, William, Jean, Isabell Hannah, Elizabeth and Eleanor. Wife, living, name not given. Died while on tour of duty in army.

Alderson, Curtis, Pro. Feb., 1804. Names wife, Elizabeth anl ch., Burr, Thomas, Elizabeth Cress, and Hester Woltz. Grandch., Elizabeth Cloyd (dau., Rachel) and Curtis Alderson, son, Thomas.

Alderson, James, dec. April, of estate returned March, 1775.

Alderson, John, Pro. Nov., 1780. Names wife, Jane, and ch., John, Curtis, Benjamin, Thomas and Simon. Grandch., George (son of John) and Thomas (son of Curtis).

Allen, Hugh, Pro. June 1776. Names wife, Anna and ch. Anne Moore, Jeny Comton, Malcolm, Thomas, William, John, James, Betsy Miller, Matilda, Polly, Robert, Patsy, Rebecca and Moses.

Allen, Malcolm. Pro. Jan., 1792. Names ch. Hugh, Robert, Moses, Rebecca, Mary, Martha, Elizabeth, Letty and John.

Allen, Moses. Pro. March, 1812. Names wife, Lydia, and ch., Polly Biggs, wife of John; Rebecca Byrd, wife of William; Malcolm (wife, Alice), and John (with wife, Martha).

Alexander, James. Pro. May, 1775. Names Mary Crawford, his cousins, James Tosh, Sarah Keachy, Thomas Tosh. Others mentioned. No relationship given.

Ammen, Durst. Pro. Sept., 1805. Names wife, Eve, and ch., Barbara, wife Christian Harshbarger; Eve, David, Jacob and Michael.

Ammen, Eve. Inv. returned Feb., 1813.

Amyx, Samuel. Pro. Jan., 1819. Names children, Isaac, Andrew, Peggy Taylor, Elizabeth Preston, Esther Lamb and Susannah and Elinor Amyx.

Anderson, William. Pro. Feb., 1820. Names wife, Nancy, and ch. Sally, Samuel, William and Alexander.

Armstrong, Elinor. Pro. April, 1791. Names ch.

Andrew, David, Robert, Alexander, Thomas, Archabald, Elinor and Isabell.

Arnold, Andrew. Pro. Feb., 1821. Names wife, Catherine, and ch. Rebekah, Abraham, David, Joseph, Jacob, Hannah, Susannah, John, Daniel and Samuel. Grandch., Peter Myers, son of Rebekah, and Mary Ann Black.

—B—

Baker, Martin, dec. Apr. estate returned July 1782.

Baldwin, Samuel. Pro. Sept., 1793. Names wife, Mary, and ch., Elizabeth, Sarah, William, Joseph, Hanna Morris, Thomas Lewis, Alexander, and ch. unnamed by his first marriage, living in Pa., except one daughter, Charity. A brother-in-law, James Wills.

Bandy, Richard. Pro. Sept., 1795. Names wife, Lucy, and ch. Thomas, Richard, John, George, Mary (wife Thomas Lewis), Eliza ("relic of Aquilla Greer"), Sarah (wife, Benj. Jordon), Katy (an infant). Also names Henry Bandy, son of Ann Bandy, presumedly a grandson.

Beale, John, dec. Dower assigned wife, Rhoda Beale, and slaves assigned his ch., Madison, George, John, Eliza, Robert, Charles and Mary Beale. March, 1811.

Beale, Madison, dec. Division of land, naming wife, Charlotte, and bro. and sisters, Charles, Mary, George, John and Eliza, wife of Thomas Lewis. May 1820.

Beale, Taverner. Will pro. June, 1810. Names wife, Betty, and heirs, Catherine, Jordon, John, Charles, James Madison Hite, Thomas and Mary Higgins.

Bear, Gothab. Will pro. April, 1814. Names Ciria Nobles - relationship not stated.

Beckner, John. Will pro. Sept., 1822. Names John Beckner's four eldest children by his first wife, Elizabeth, viz: David, Catherin, Mary and John. Also his bros. and sisters, unnamed.

Beckner, Lawrence. Pro. Oct., 1802. Names ch., Jonathan, Daniel, Jacob, Elizabeth, Simmons, Susannah Garmon and John.

Beldin, Hezekiah. Pro. Oct., 1809. Names

bros., William and Samuel of Conn.

Bilbro, Betsy. Pro. July, 1811. Names niece, Rebekah Carey, and a bro., William Carey.

Bilbro, William. Pro. Oct. 1807. Names wife, Mary, and ch., Sarah Terril (of Elk River), Rebecca Wallace, Betsy, Rachel, John, James, Benjamin, and Thomas. Grandch., Rebecca Sulla and William Carey.

Bishop, Jeremiah. Pro. May, 1820. Non-cupative will. One third to wife, and bal. to ch., Abram and Mary Conner.

Black, Christian. Pro. Aug., 1812. Names wife, Franche, and ch., unnamed except one, Elizabeth.

Blain, William, dec. Apr of estate returned, June, 1819.

Blount, Wilson. Pro. Oct., 1819. Names friend, Wm. Shepherd, of Newburn, nephews, Ebeneazer Petegrew, Frederick Beasley, Clement Blount. Niece, Sarah Fuller, and grandniece, Nancy B. Petticrew, who, he states, is the dau. of William Shepherd.

Boindrager, Andrew, dec. Estate inv. Aug, 1815.

Boindrager, William. Pro. Oct., 1798. Names wife, Susanna, and ch., Nancy, Martin, Susanna Pefley, and David.

Bowyer, Thomas. Pro. Aug., 1785. Names Pricilla Madison, and a nephew, Henry Bowyer.

Boyd, Andrew. Pro. June, 1820. Names ch., John, Thomas, Sarah, Ann Buchanon, Margaret, Pricilla ("my unfortunate dau"), Alexander. The heirs of a dec. child, Mary and James.

Boyd, Andrew. Pro. Feb., 1821. Names wife, and ch., Andrew, Margaret, Mary and James.

Boyd, James. Will pro. July, 1816. Names wife, Mary, and ch., Andrew and William Watson.

Breckenridge, Robert. Pro. Nov. 7, 1773. Names wife, Lettice, and ch., William John, Alexander, Robert, James, Preston and Elizabeth.

Brown, Hugh. Pro. Feb., 1802. Names ch., Mary Moore, Sarah Wilson, Jane Taylor, Paggy Brown, Nancy Brown, John, and Hugh, the last "whereabouts unknown."

Brown, James, dec. Inv. returned, Sept. 1812.

Brown, Thomas. Pro. Aug., 1823. Names ch., Esther, Rebecca, Massa, Kezia, Mary Thompson, William and Thomas. (His dec. wife was dau. Wm. Terry.)

Brugh, Harmon. Pro. Oct., 1794. Names wife, Catherine, and ch., John (eldest), Jacob, Daniel, Harmon, Cathren (wife, Henry

Neil), Mary (wife, John Stouffer). Will signed in German.

Brunk, John, dec. Inv. of estate returned, May, 1811.

Bryan, William. Pro. Oct., 1806. Names wife, Elizabeth, and ch., William, Catherine Cole, James and John.

Buchannon, Theadore. Pro. Oct., 1814. Speaks of wife, two sons and a dau. No names.

Bumbgardner, Paulser, dec. Sales bill ret. Dec. 1822.

Burwell, Lewis. Pro. Oct., 1804. Names bro. and sisters. Gives namse of only two, Nathaniel and Frances. Speaks of dec. father, Nathaniel, and dec. uncle, Lewis Burwell.

—C—

Caldwell, John. Pro. April, 1820. Names wife, Susannah, and ch., William, Rosannah, Sarah, Jane, Archibald, Nancy, John, Joseph, Susannah, and Robert.

Caldwell, Mary. Pro. April, 1814. Names ch. Granvill, John (and his dau., Sally), Edmison, Samuel, and the heirs of dec. dau., Jane. Granddau., Mary Mcferran. A brother, Hugh.

Caldwell, Robert, dec. Apr. of estate, Feb., 1790.

Campbell, Archibald. Pro. April 1774. Names his bro., William (and his eldest son). Two sons of Wm. Sompson, John and Archibald. A sister, Jean, but disinherits her she marry Nathaniel Evans, the bro. of Peter.

Campbell, Arthur, dec. Apr. of estate ret. March, 1775.

Campbell, Willaim. Pro. Sept., 1818. Names wife, Magdalene, and nine bros. and sisters - no names given.

Campbell, William. Pro. Oct., 1804. Names wife, Susannah, and ch., Thomas, Archibald, William, James, John, Rhoda and Polly. Leaves his sons "land in the western country."

Camper, Peter, dec. Inv. of estate ret. Jan., 1789.

Camper, Solomon. Pro. Jan., 1824. Names wife, Lessaley, and heirs. Thomas Grimes, Mary Ann Croft, Lydia Falls, Harmon, Lilly C., Lucy Leadin, Lucy Camper, Bussey, Valentine G., and the heirs of a dec. son, John.

Carlton, William. Pro. Sept., 1813. Names ch. Henry, William, Joseph, Rebecca Thomas, Mary, Susannah, James. Grandch., William and Susanna Pawley.

Carpenter, Leah. Pro. Sept., 1806. Names ch.,

Judy Shaver; grandch. Polly Gillespie, and Becky and Leah Shawver.

Carpenter, Joseph. Pro. July, 1792. Names wife, Leah, and ch., Abagail Maloney, Mary Viers, Sarah Gillespie, Judy Shawver, Marthew, Samuel and William.

Carper, Nicholas. Will pro. May, 1813. Names wife, Elizabeth, and ch., Jacob, Benjamin, Elizabeth Harvey Mary Mcferran, Joseph, Sally, Holestine and Isaac.

Carrigan, Patrick, Will pro. Jan., 1795. Names wife, Mary, and "my beloved relation, Jacob Carrigan," son of Michael, of Pa.

Cartmell, Henry. Will pro. Feb. 13, 1787. Names wife, Mary, and ch., Henry, Jr., John, and James Sons-in-law, James Green, William Patterson, James Huston and Robert Stewart and Robert's son, Henry.

Carvin, Richard. Will pro. Nov., 1823. Names wife, Lucy.

Carvin, William. Will pro. Sept., 1804. Names wife, ..., and ch., Elwarl, Elizabeth, Richard, Mary, Nancy Alley.

Chenowith, Thomas. Will pro. une, 1780. Names wife, Ann, and ch., Elizabeth, Mary, James, Francis, Thomas, John, and Nicholas Raveton.

Christian, Elizabeth. Will pro. Sept., 1789. Names ch., Anne (wife, Col. Wm. Fleming), and gr.ch., Elizabeth Fleming and Fleming, Stephen, Mary and Elizabeth Trigg.

Circle, Peter. Will pro. Oct., 1818. Names wife, Fanny, and ch., Andrew ,Mathias, Emanuel, Lewis, John, Peter and sons-in-law, Peorge Knisley, Jacob Knisley, Isaac France, John Nicenger, and Christley Fisher.

Clear, George, dec. Apr. of estate ret. Sept., 1790.

Cleck, Baldas. Will pro. Dec., 1803. Names wife, Sophia, and ch., John, Margaret, Christinah, Jacob, and Elizabeth.

Cloyd, Michael. Will pro. April, 1807. Names ch., John, David, Michael, Samuel, Joseph, (land on Cloyd's st. Amsterdam), Jesse and Elizabeth Law (land on Round st., Amsterdam).

Cockran, Peter, dec. Aprl ret. July, 1771.

Cofmon, Henry, dec. Inv. ret May, 1804.

Coffman, Jacob. Will pro. June, 1807. Names wife, Barbra, and ch., Benjamin, John, Fanny Hanes and Jacob.

Compton, John, dec. Inv. ret. Sept,. 1778.

Coon, Michael. Will pro. 1813. Names wife, Doratha, and ch., John, Eve (wife John Ship), Catherine (wife Mitchael Davis), Sarah (wife Wm. Ireland), Rosannah (wife

Andrew Zimmerman), Doratha (wife Amry Seacrist), Elizabeth (wife, John Kelly) and Jacob. Ch. of dec. son, Adam.

Cooper, James. Will pro. Dec., 1784. Names wife and ch. No names given.

Cox, Edward, dec. Inv. of estate ret. May, 1784.

Crawford, Andrew. Will pro. Feb., 1791. Names wife, Ufree, and ch., John, James Eunice.

Crawford, John (son of John). Will pro. June 1796. Names wife, Margaret, and ch. John, William, Andrew, James, Samuel, Margaret. Also his bro., William.

Critts, George. Will pro. June, 1805. Names wife, Mary, and ch., John, Elizabeth, Conrad, Mary, George, Tunay, Anney, Catey, Henry and Philip.

Cross, William. Will pro. June, 1798. Names wife, Elizabeth, and ch., Wm., Jr., Mary, Jane, John and Elizabeth Eath.

Crouse, Daniel. Will pro. Oct., 1818. Names wife, Catherine, and dau. Anny.

Cunningham, Hugh. Will pro. May, 1772. Names wife, Sarah, and ch., Jezabel, and ten others - names not given. A stepson, James Davis, and a son-in-law, John Young.

—D—

Darick, John. Will pro. Sept., 1790. Names wife, Mary, and ch., but no names given, except "my little son, Jonathan."

Davidson, William. Will pro. Oct., 1812. Names wife, Martha, and ch., Ginny M'Cartney, Joseph, and three other daus., no names given.

Deardroff, Henry, dec. Apr. of estate ret. Feb. 1792.

Deaton, Martha, dec. Inv. of estate ret. May, 1822.

Dennis, Joseph. Will pro. June, 1794. Names wife, and ch. No names given.

Dennison, John, dec. Apr. of estate ret, May, 1776.

Depew, John. Will pro. Sept., 1811. Names wife, Catherine, and ch., Elijah, Isaac (eldest), Lawerecia Datzell, Abraham, James, John, and Jacob. The heirs of a dec. son, Samuel, and a granddau., child of his son, James.

Depew, Samuel, dec. Apr. of estate ret. Jan., 1792.

Detzell, James. Will pro. Sept., 1815. Names wife, Martha, and ch., James, Hugh, Nancy, Sally, and Betsy.

Dill, Henry. Will pro. June, 1818. Names wife,

Thrias*, and ch., Andrew, Esther, Susanna, Ann (wife, Abraham Brubaker), and sons-in law, Daniel Dilman and Michael Rule. *In settlement of estate wife's name is given as Mary.

Dilmon, Daniel, dec. Sale recorded Dec., 1819.

Dodd, William. Will pro. Dec., 1822. Names wife, Mary, and ch., Thomas, Sally Hipes, William and John. A grandson, Adney Dodd.

Dollman, Henry. Division of land. June, 1824. Names widow Sarah, and ch., Sarah, Nancy (wife of Philip Snider), Barbara (wife, George Knode), Mary, Eve and Catherine.

Douglas, Benjamin. Will pro. June, 1816. Names wife, Charity, and ch., James, John, William, Francis, Elizabeth Saintclair, Behethelon Monson, Benjamin, Gideon and Mary Anderson.

Dryden, Thomas. Will pro. April 1777. Names wife, Agnes, and ch., Nathaniel, David, Thomas, and others, no or names not given.

Duncan, Robert. Will pro. June 1787. Names wife, Cattron, and ch., Mary, Eastair, Rachel, Robert. Nancy, Margaret, Elizabeth, Rebecca, Isabel and Janet.

—E—

Egar, Martha. Will pro. April, 1789. Names "my beloved child, Jane Logan." Bequeaths to her "one horse, one calico gown, one stiff gown, a silk bunnit, a cotton handkerchief, a silk ditto, and all that she was to get of Moses Egers estate."

Eakins, Nathan. Will pro. 1823. Names wife, Susannah, and ch., Thomas, William, Mary Rice, Nathan, Nancy Walker, Samuel, Stephen, Joseph, John, Rebekah, Susannah, Equilla Broyles (who is separated from her husband, Solomon), and Preston.

Eakin, Thomas. Will pro. Feb., 1810. Names wife, Agnes, and ch., Joseph, William and Thomas.

Eakin, William, dec. Inv. returned Sept., 1815.

Eason, Francis. Will pro. Aug. 1788. Names ch., Samuel, Joseph, Nancy and Elizabeth. Says the two daughters are now "in captivity," but provides for them should they ever be found.

Emack, Matthew, "yeoman." Will pro. April, 1779. Names sons, James, Matthew, and Samuel. A son-in-law, James Smith.

Evans, Peter. Will pro. Jan. 1797. Names wife, Mary, and ch., Mark, Thomas, Jonathan, William, John, Betsy, and Catron.

Evans, Thomas. Will pro. March, 1785. Names

friends, James Gost, David Porter and James Pergrain.

—F—

Ferrel, Gabriel. Will pro. Jan., 1803. Names wife, Anna, and ch., Elizabeth, Milly Hanes, Abner and Stephen.

Francisco, Ludewick. Will pro. April, 1799. Names wife, Elizabett, and ch., Jacob, George, Elizabeth, Ester, Christina, Margaret, Lodewick, Susanna, Mary and Sarah.

Frantz, Christian, dec. Inv. of estate ordered Dec., 1822.

Frantz, Michael. Will pro. May, 1817. Names wife, Elizabeth, and ch., Michael (of Ky.), Elizabeth (wife Adam Shanks, of Ky.), Catherine (wife of Henry Britz), and Polly (wife of Daniel Stover).

Firestone, Nicholas. Will pro. Nov., 1808. Names wife, Eve Catherine, and ch., John, Eve (wife, John), Nicholas, Magdalene (wife John Wren), Susanna (wife Philip Hyleman), Elizabeth, Catherine (wife Chas. Long), and Matthias.

Fleming, William. Will pro. Oct., 1795. Names ch., Leonard Israel Christian, Elizabeth (wife, Cary H. Allen), Dorthea (land in By.), William, John, Annie, Christian and Pricilla.

Freeman, Derry. Will pro. Sept., 1804. Names wife, Peggy, and a son, Isaac.

Fulhart, Henry. Will pro. Feb., 1819. Names wife, Mary, and sons, John and Henry.

—G—

Galloway, Robert. Will pro. Aug., 1779. Names wife, Elinor, and ch., David, John, Esebell, William, Jean, Mary and Robert.

Garmon, John. Will pro. Sept., 1799. Names wife, Susanna, and ch., Adam and Mary Elizabeth.

Garst, Nicholas. Will pro. Oct., 1803. Names wife, Mary, and ch. - names or number not given, except one son, John Nicholas.

Garwood, Joseph. Will pro. June, 1823. Names wife, Martha, and ch., Samuel (land in Ky.), Sarah, Elizabeth, Peggy and John.

Gatty, John. Will pro. April, 1801. Names bros., Dennis, Jerry, Jeremiah. A sister, Bridget, and two other sisters in Ireland. Names not given.

Gaunt, James, dec. Inv. of estate ret, Hept., 1778.

Gentry, John. Will pro. May, 1779. Names wife, Mary, and ch., no or names not given.

Gerard, John, dec. Apr. of estate Dec., 1807.

Wife, Rachel.

Getty, Dennis, dec. Apr. of estate ret. Aug., 1779.

Gilleland, James. Will pro. April, 1811. Names wife, Susannah, and ch., Sally Shepherd, Joseph, James, Betsy, Mary, John, William, Samuel, Tency, Nancy and Susannah.

Gillespy, Hugh, dec. Inv. of estate ret.March, 1777.

Gillespy, Robert. Will pro. April, 1798. Names ch., William, Isabel, Mary, Robert, John, James, Alexander and Jean. Grandson, John Gillespy.

Gillespy, Simon, dec. Apr. ret. Nov., 1821. Wife, Nancy.

Gish, Christian. Will pro June, 1796. Names wife, Sophia, and ch., Christian, Elizabeth, Caty, George, Abraham, Jacob and others, names or no. not given.

Givens, Daniel. Will pro. March, 1823. Names ch., Anna Webb, Susanna, wife, John Walker; Oilinda Peck, William, Isiah, Elisha, Joseph and Daniel. Grandch., Daniel (Wm's son), and Patsy Peck, dau. Jacob Peck.

Glenn, Jean, lec. Apr. of estate ret. Aug., 1803.

Gortner, Catherine, dec. Apr. of estate ret. Sept, 1819.

Gortner, Philip. Settlement of estate prior to above. Names widow, Catherine, and Charlotte Mallow (wife, Michael), Mary, Jacob (wife, Catherine), Elizabeth, John and Mary (wife Joseph Key).

Goulding, Thomas (of Rockbridge). Will pro. May, 1778. Names Thomas Goulding of Long Bay, N. C.

Graham, William. Will pro. Sept., 1786. Names wife, Elizabeth, and ch., Elizabeth, wife Joseph Robinson; Francis, Nancy, wife of Walter Greer; Catherine, wife Edward Springer and George.

Green, George, dec. Div. of estate Oct., 1784. Names heirs, Thomas M'Clanahan, John Reburn, John and Janet Green.

Greenwood, William. Will pro. Oct., 1812. Names wife, Jane, and ch., Robert, Margaret, Jane and Mary.

Gregor, Christine. Will pro. Jan., 1809. Names grandch., Rebecca and John Gregor (see Grogan).

Greybill, John. Will pro. Sept., 1818. Names wife, Hannah, and ch., John, Daniel, Solomon, Elizabeth, wife John Fisher, and Shem. Sons-in-law, Daniel Arnold and Jacob Garmon.

Grist, John, dec. Apr. returned Oct., 1791.

Grogan, John. Will pro. Dec., 1803. Names wife, Christine.

Gross, Jacob, dec. Inv. ret. Dec., 1804.

Gross, Martin, dec. Dower assigned widow, Margaret, Feb., 1798.

Gulliford, Allen. Will pro. Oct., 1815. Names wife, Anna, and ch., Henry, Anderson, Pricilla, Elizabeth Wilson, James and Allen.

Gurney, Henry (of Pa.). Will pro. June, 1792. Names Elizabeth Doughty, "brought up by him," a sister, Elizabeth Brookfield, nephew, Stephen Tucker, and two nieces, Catherine, named.

—H—

Hall, William. Will pro. Feb., 1773. Names wife, Jean, and ch., Andrew, Agnes Berry, John, Isabel Buchanan, William, Nathaniel and James. Grandch., William and James, sons of Andrew.

Hamilton, Andrew. Will pro. Nov., 1823. Names wife ...., and ch., James, Alexander, Wilson Cary, and daus., no. or names not given.

Hamilton, Godfrey. Will pro. July, 1795. Names Catherine and Wm. Koger, ch., Peter Koger.

Hamilton, John. Will pro. May, 1811. Names ch., James, John (land in Ky), and others, no. or names not given.

Hamilton, John. Will pro. May, 1823. Names Ch., John, William, Samuel, Mary Croft, Susannah and Margaret.

Hammon, Peter, dec. Adm. appointed. Wife, Barbara. March, 1822.

Handley, Alexander. Will pro. Sept., 1781. Names wife, Mary, and ch. "little daughter, Martha Breaker," and one other, name not given. Bro.-in-law, Wm. Ewing.

Hannah, Alexander. Will pro. Sept., 1820. Names wife, Mary, and ch., James, Joseph, Peggy Gibson, and Anna Taylor.

Hanson, David. Will pro. Jan., 1800. Names wife, ... and ch., Samuel, Daniel, Mary Bags, and Marcha. G.ch., Annie, Elizabeth and Sally Caldwell, daus. John. Disinherits son, Samuel, should he marry Rachel Gulliver.

Harbison, William. Will pro. March, 1775. Names wife, Mary, and ch., Davil, Hannah, William, George, Agnes, Mary, Jean, Grizzle, Rebecca, Elizabeth. Son-in-law, Nathaniel Evans.

Harmon, Jacob. Will pro. Aug., 1792. Names wife, Margareta, and ch., John, Lewis, Jacob, Margareta, Elizabeth and Catherine Mase.

Harmon, John, dec. Apr. of estate ret. May, 1778.

Harmantrout, George. Will pro. Oct., 1798. Names wife, Barbary, son, Frederick, and heirs of dec. daughter, Catherine Russell, viz: George, Mary and Catherine.

Harrison, John, dec. Inv. estate ret. Aug., 1786.

Harshbarger, Mary. Will pro. Dec., 1802. Names ch., Christley, Jacob and Samuel.

Harvey, Matthew. Will pro. Nov., 1823. Names wife, Maglalena, and ch., Lucy Magdalene, Frances, Jane, Elizabeth, Virginia, Polly (wife, Robert Kyle), Mary H. (wife Wm. A. McDowell), and John.

Hawk, James. Will pro. Jan., 1824. Names friends, Edmund Richeson and Peter Keyfogger.

Hawkins, Benjamin. Will pro. May, 1779. Names wife, Martha, and ch., William, James, John, Borden, Magdalen, and Sarah.

Haynes, John. Will pro. June, 1797. Names wife, Jannet, and ch., Jannet Harriet, Granville, William Henry, Ann Gulleland, Elizabeth Holeday, and Agnes Kitchen. A bro., William.

Haynes, Nicholas. Wll pro. June, 1797. Names wife, Elizabeth, and ch., Isaac, John, Margaret Miffert, Catherine Luder, Christopher and Jacob.

Hays, John. Will pro. Nov., 1822. Names ch., John, Thomas, Jonathan, Ruth and Lewis. Gr.ch., James, son of Thomas; Harrison, son of Jonathan; and Henry, son of Lewis.

Hazelwood, Joshua, dec. Apr. ret. Feb., 1812.

Heavins, John. Will pro. Aug., 1784. Names wife, Sarah, and ch., James, Mary (wife, Thomas Finley of N. C.), Howard and John.

Henry, William, dec. Inv. of estate ret. June, 1816.

Hewett, John, dec. Inv. ret. Sept., 1812.

Hill, Edward, dec. Venue bill ret. April, 1811.

Himes, John. Will pro. Jan., 1808. Names ch., John, Isaac, David, Elizabeth, Barbary, Abraham and Daniel - the youngest.

Hindmon, John, dec. Settlement of est. Feb., 1798.

Hiner, John. Will pro. Dec., 1801. Names wife, Mary, and ch., Henry (eldest son), Gertrude (eldest dau. and wife of Solomon Letts), Catey, Polly (wife Samuel Nofsinger), Elizabeth, Susannah, Abraham, John, Peter and Anthony.

Hiner, Peter, dec. Dower assigned Catherine Fellers, former wife, Dec., 1823. Heirs named: Anthony, John, Peter Hiner; P. Beard's

wife, J. Boyd's wife, and John Moore's wife.

wife, Apolonia, and ch., John, Peter, Henry, Maria, Elizabeth Able, Barbara, "late Hammon", Magdaline Gross and Margaret.

Hively, Jacob, dec. Adm. of estate Aug., 1819.

Hof, Lewis. Will pro. Aug., 1823. Names wife, Rachel, and ch., Abraham, Daniel, David, Peter, Catrina, John, Maryan and Samuel.

Hoffes, Nicholas, dec. Apr. of estate Sept. 1802.

Houtz, Jacob, dec. Adm. of estate apt. His wife, Polly Houtz, 1818.

Howard, Edward. Will pro. May, 1785. Names wife, Elizabeth, and son, Ezekiel.

Howell, Abner. Will pro. Sept., 1812. Names wife, Hannah, and ch., James, Samuel, Thomas, Jesse, David, Jemima Rader, Mary Gish and Ruth Gish.

Howery, Jacob, dec. Apr. ret. Dec., 1809.

Huddle, George. Will pro. Sept., 1794. Names wife, Margaret, and ch., George, Elizabeth and Christian - all minors.

Hugart, William, dec. Inv. of estate ret. May, 1775.

Hutchinson, William. Will pro. April, 1778. Names kinsman, James Hutchinson, Sr.

—I—

Inglebird, George, dec. Est. settled, May, 1778.

Ingram, Alexander. Will pro. May, 1778. Names wife, Mary, and ch., Ann (married), John, William, James, Mary and Alexander, Jr.

—J—

Janhoward, Samuel. Will pro. Dec., 1824. Names wife, Ann, and ch., John, Thomas Jefferson, Timothy Newel, Cynthia Magdalene (wife, Henry W. Kelly), Jacob, Betsy Cahoon, Susan Camper, Samuel and Barbara.

Jenkins, Jeremiah. Will pro. Feb., 1821. Names Elinor Felts and her sons, Peter and Benjamin. Also Amelia Williams; no relationship stated.

John, Jacob. Will pro. Oct., 1806. Names wife, Cathren, and ch., Henry and Jacob. Son-in-law, Daniel Bare. One dollar to ch. of first marriage, unnamed.

Johnston, Eve. Will pro. Nov., 1809. Names heirs, Henry Persinger, Jacob Johnston, William Johnston, Sarah Porter, Rachel Linkhorn, and Margaret Smith. Gr.dau., Rebecca Smith.

Johnston, Ezekiel. Will pro. Aug., 1781. Names a wife, Eve, and ch., Andrew, Sarah, Rachel,

John, Jacob, William and Margaret.

Johnston, Peter, dec. Apr. ret. Dec., 1794.

Jones, Ambrois. Will pro. May, 1822. Names wife, Elizabeth, and ch., Polly, Allen, Ambroise, Catherine Moyer, Milly Watkins, Mary Watkins (her heirs), Nancy Watkins (her heirs), and Sally Russall.

Jones, John. Will pro. July, 1773. Names wife, Elizabeth, and ch., Nathaniel, John, Margaret McCoy, Elizabeth, John, Marthew, Sarah, Jean, Hannah, wife of Thomas Harrison.

Jones, John Gabriel. Will pro. Nov., 1779. Names brothers, Samuel (a surgeon), Gabriel, and Thomas. A bro-in-law, Thomas Griffith; a friend, Patrick, Lockhart. Sisters, Elizabeth, Ann, Margaret, Charlotte Griffith - property in England. His father was John Jones. Grandfather, Samuel Slade, both of England.

—K—

Keefauver, Katherine. Will pro. Jan., 1820. Names ch., Mary and Elizabeth.

Kent, Jacob. Will pro. Feb. 1, 1777. Names wife, Mary, and ch., John, Joseph, Robert, Jacob, Jane and Nancy.

Keslar, Jacob. Will pro. Sept., 1824. Names wife, Elizabeth, and ch. George, John, Jacob, Henry, Catherine, Daniel, Andrew, Benjamin, David, Samuel and Elizabeth.

Kilmer, George. Will pro. March, 1823. Names wife, Catherine, and ch., Elizabeth Hammel, Susanna Eve Cup, Marbary Magdalene Johnson, Esther, Margaret, William, Nancy, Sarah and George.

Kimberling, Paulzer. Will pro. Oct., 1808. Names wife, Sarah, and ch., James, Martha Matthews, Agnes Pitzer, Rebecca Pitzer, John and Jacob.

Kinny, John. Will pro. Nov., 1813. Names wife, Elizabeth, and ch., William, James, Joseph, David, Sampson, John, Sally Betsy, and Susanna.

Kinny, William. Will pro. Nov., 1774. Names wife, Elizabeth, anl ch., James, Agnes, Jean, Elizabeth, Marrey.

Kitchen, Henry, dec. Apr. of estate, Jan., 1792.

Kyle, Archibald. Will pro. March, 1784. Names wife, Mary, and ch., Sally, Rhoda, Fanny and Marvin.

Kyle, Jane. Will pro. Nov., 1820. Names ch., Christopher, Jane Pitzer, Robert and Dinguid.

Kyle, Joseph. Will pro., 1808. Names wife, Jane, and ch., Robert, Dinguid, William, Christopher, Anne, Elizabeth, Polly, Jane,

Patsy, Martha. Names of daus. not in will. Shown in settlement.

Kyle, Mary, dec. Settlement of est., Sept., 1784.

Kyle, Nancy, dec. Apr. ret. Oct., 1811.

Kyle, William. Will pro. Dec., 1809. Names bros., Christopher, Robert, Dinguid, his mother, Jane Kyle. (He was son of Joseph, dec.)

Kyle, William. Names wife, Sarah, and ch., Jane Womack, Barclay, Sally Rowland and James. Sons-in-law, John Dickerson and Charles Beale. Grandsons, James Pitzer (born Oct., 1805), and Rboert Pitzer (born Dec., 1807), both sons of George Pitzer.

—L—

Lackey, James. Will pro. Oct., 1823. Names wife, Mary, and ch., Thomas, Nathan, Martha McKnight, Mary and Samuel.

Lange, Christian Chas. Will pro. Aug., 1817. Names wife, Elizabeth, and wife's sister, Christina Schlengliss.

Lantz, Peter, dec. Inv. ret. Nov., 1822.

Lawyers, Sacpson. Will pro. April, 1819. Names wife, Mary, and ch., Andrew, Matthew, Rebeccah, Alexander and Archer.

Larkins, Henry. Will pro. Feb., 1773. Names wife, Jain, and ch., James, Henry, Mary, David, Thomas, Elizabeth, Sarah, Jain, Margaret, Nancy and Marthew.

Lawrence, James, Jr. Will pro. Nov., 1773. Names wife, Frances, and daughter, Elizabeth. Also, brothers, Henry Hunter, William, Samuel, David, John, Solomon, Isaac, Joseph and Robert.

Leforce, Rene, dec. Apr. ret. Oct., 1781.

Lemmon, George, Sr. Will pro. April, 1807. Names wife, Elizabeth, and "third son, Jacob." Other sons, but names not given.

Lester, Nancy. Will pro. Sept., 1823. Names ch., Polly and John. Others, but names not given.

Lewis, Andrew. Will pro. Feb., 1782. Names wife, and ch., John, Samuel, Thomas, Andrew, William, Anne. Gr.sons, Andrew, Samuel, and Charles (sons of John). Bros., Thomas and William .Sister, Margaret.

Lewis, Andrew, dec. Div. estate, 1821. Names heirs as John, William, Patsy, Samuel, Emil, Eliza, and Jane Anne Lewis, and Sally, wife, James L. Woods.

Lewis, John. Will pro. Aug., 1782. Names wife, Marthew, and ch., Andrew, Samuel, Charles, Elizabeth and one unborn.

Likins Andrew, dec. Apr. ret. Nov., 1781.

Lindsey, Margaret. Will pro. April, 1804.

Names sons, Samuel, Matthew, and Walter; gr.ch., Samuel (son, Walter), Samuel (son Nathan), Margaret (dau, Walter), and Margaret and Samuel Cantley. A niece, Agnes Smithey.

Linknhonger, Elias, dec. Adm ret. Dec., 1822. Settlement of est, names ch., George, Lydia Spiller, Catherine Bourn, Anna Riddlebarger, Elias, Hannah Sifford, Sarah Kiser, Joseph, Betsy, John, Rebecca Boose, and Adam. Wife, dec., was Hannah.

Linkenhonger, Elizabeth, dec. Inv., ret,, Dec. 1822.

Little David. Will pro. Dec., 1813. Names ch. John, Robert, William, James, David, Sarah, and Rebeccah.

Little, John. Will pro. July, 1793. Names wife, Elizabeth, and ch. David, John, William, Mary, Fanny and Sarah. "Males to have 20 shillings each, and females, 15 shillings".

Little William, dec. Apr. of estate Sept, 1819.

Logan, John, dec. Apr. ret., March, 1773.

Long, Elizabeth, Will pro. Jan., 1824. Names friend, Peter Bush.

Looney, Absolum, Will pro. June, 1796. Names ch. Michael, Elizabeth Potts, Peter, Mary Swanson, Margaret Caldwell, Jonathan, Absolum, Ruth, Ann Harberson, Catherine, Pricilla Caldwell and Benjamin.

Looney, John, dec. Div. est. Dec., 1823. Named widow, Elizabeth and ch. Sarah, Joseph, John, and William Looney. Widow remarried this date to Reynolds.

Looney Robert. Will pro. Nov., 1770. Wife, Elizabeth, and ch.; Joseph, and others, no names or number.

Loop Philip, Will pro. Oct., 1824. Names wife, Catherine, and ch. Sarah, Simon, Christian, Catherine, John Jacob, Rebecca' Barbara, Philip, Elizabeth and Susanna.

Love, Philip, dec. Inv. ret. Jan., 1793.

Lyth, John, Will pro. Dec., 1781. Names Mrs. Betsy Breckenridge. Made when leaving home for army.

—M—

Madison, John. Will pro. March, 1784. Names wife, Agatha, and ch. Rowland, George, Thomas, dau.-i-law, Elizabeth, widow of dec. son, William, and her ch., Elizabeth Smith Madison, and Agatha Strother Madison. A dau-in-law, Susanna Madison, and son-in-law, Andrew Lewis.

Madison, Thomas. Will pro. Sept., 1798. Names wife, Susannah, and ch. Agatha,

wife Col. Bowyer; John H., Thomas, Patrick, Peggy Sale Annie, and Jennie.

Mann, William ,Will pro. Nov., 1778. Names wife Jeane, and ch. Moses, Thomas, William, John, Catie, Jenny, Sarah and one unborn.

Mann, Wm., dec. Inv. ret. Feb., 1795.

Markey, Nicholas. Will pro. Feb. 1824. Names wife, Barbara, and ch. George, and others unnamed. A brother David Markey, of Pa.

Martin, Johnson. Will pro. June, 1818. Names wife, , and ch., Nancy Bartel, Judy, Sarah, and Feby.

Martin Josiah, dec. Dower assigned wife, Polly, Nov., 1820.

Matthews William. Will pro. Nov., 1772. Names wife, Frances, and ch. Ann, Elizabeth, John, Joseph and James. Brothers Samson and George Matthews.

Mason, James. Will pro. 1808. Names ch. of Samuel and Janet Crawford (of Ky.); viz, William, Samuel, Mason, Jane Pate, Elinor Jennings, Margaret and Sarah Crawford. (Said Janet "his sister and best friend"). Also heirs of his bro, Wm; his sister Mary Eager, of Bedford; sister, Margaret Snodgrass, of Tenn. and a bro. Joseph of Breckenridge, Ky.

Mason, Martin, dec. apr. ret. Dec. 1794. Settlement of estate lists ch. as: William, Daniel, John, Jonathan, Martin. Abraham, Catherine Elizabeth, Mary ,Peggy Susanna, Sara, and Nancy Made. June, 1815. (O. B. 1818-15.)

Maura, Conrad. Will pro. Feb., 1824. Names son, Conrad, of Somerset co. Pa., and son-in-law, Henry Painter.

Mays, Mary. Will pro. May, 1822. Names ch., Susannah Tate, Mary Cross, and James Mays.

Maze, William. Will pro. March, 1783. Names wife, Margaret, and ch. William, Richard, Sarah McMurray and Mrry Scott.

McCarty, Nancy. Will pro. Nov., 1823. Names sister, Elizabeth Kidd, (her dau. Eliz.), of King and Queen Co., and bro. and sister, John and Luray Campbell. A niece, Susan, of bro. John.

McClanahan, Robert, dec. Inv. ret. 1774.

McClanahan, Washington. dec. Settlement of estate, Sept., 1819'

McClanahan, William. Will pro. Nov. 1819. Names wife, Sarah, and ch. Elijah, James and Green. The widow and sons, Wm .and Chas., of son John. Heirs of dec. son, Washington. Wife, Elizabeth, and ch.

Washington and John, of son, Green, Gr. ch. William McClanahan, William Lewis Cok, William Lewis Jr., William McClanahan Jr., and m. Markle.

McClung, John. Will pro. May, 1779. Names bro. James, and sister, Agnes Gray.

McClure, John. Will pro. Feb. 1778. Names wife, and ch. Samuel, Alexander, Mary, Agnes, Jannet, Malcolm, Hannah, Rebeccah, John, Holbert, Moses and Nathaniel.

McClure, Malcolm. Will pro. June 1791. Names wife, Elizabeth, and ch. John and Mary. A bro. Samuel and nephew, Samuel Jr.

McConnell, James. Will pro. June, 1813. Names wife, Nancy and ch. James, Peter, Jessy, and heirs of dec. son, John.

McConnell, James. Will pro. May, 1821. Leaves estate to friends.

McConnell Nancy. Will pro. Sept, 1818. Names ch. Peter and James.

McCown, Patrick. dec. Apr. of estate Dec. 1772.

McCreary, John, dec. Apr. ret. Oct., 1802.

McDonald Bryam. Will pro. Feb 1777. Names wife Susannah, a nd ch. James, William, Thomas, Edward, George' Mary Susannah, and Jane.

McDonald James. Will pro. March, 1778. Names mother, Susannah, and sisters and bros. Edward, William, George, Mary, Susannah and Jean.

McFerran Archibald. Will pro. Aug. 1777. Names bro. Isaac, "can he be found", and uncle, John McFerran, of county Derby, Ireland.

McFerran James. Will pro. Sept., 1806. Names mother, Anne McFerran.

McFerrand, John. Will pro. May, 1776. Names wife, Margaret, and ch. Samuel, (with son, Robert), John, James and Thomas. A gr. son, John McFerrand.

McFerran, Martin. Will pro. Feb. 1816. Names Hetty and Martin McFerran, the ch. of Samuel McFerran of Tenn.

McFerron, Samuel. Will pro. Feb. 1820. Names wife, and ch. Ann and Martin. His mother, unnamed, and niece Hetty McFerron.

McGraw Brien, dec. Inv. ret. June 15, 1771.

McKeechy James. Will pro. Sept. 1805. Names wife, Rebecca, and son Andrew.

McKnight George. Will pro. Aug. 1815. Names ch. James, Jean, Sarah, William, Elizabeth, Nancy, John, George and Thomas.

McMath, William. Will pro. Oct. 1782. Names wife, Margaret, a bro. James, and James' son, William.

McMullin, Edward. Will pro. June 1788. Names wife, Sarah, and ch., John, (eldest), Elizabeth, Margaret and Agnes (by a first wife). James, Edward, Joseph Samuel, Sampson, Lovia, Jean, Esther, Sarah, Lettice and Mary, ch. of 2nd marriage.

McMurray, William, dec. Adm. of est. ret. 1798.

McNeal, Daniel. Will pro. Aug. 1818. Names wife, Sarah, and ch. Jane (wife Robt. Filson), Polly (wife Geo Bright), and grandson, Thomas Jefferson Bright.

McNeal, Hugh. Will pro. Feb. 1796. Names wife, Martha, and ch., Mary McGlaughlin, Lida Gordon, Martha Murphy, John, Sarah, Duke, Margaret and Elizabeth.

McNeal, James,. Will pro. Nov., 1778. Names wife, Mary, and ch., Joseph and Mary. Bro. Jonathan.

McNeal, John. Will pro. Feb. 1773. Names wife, Mary, and ch., Rebeckah, Nancy Mary, Sarah, and one unborn.

McNeel, John. dec. Apr. ret. Dec. 1789.

Marrett, Samuel. dec. Apr. ret. Sept. 1821.

Mifford, Jacob. Will pro. June 1798. Names wife, Peggy, and ch. Elizabeth Nugent, Polly, John, Jacob, Catherine, Peggy and Pricilla.

Miller, David, dec. Hannah, wife, made adm. Sept. 1811.

Mills, Hugh. Will pro. May., 1785. Names bros. Blaney and John, and John's son, Hugh.

Mills, John, dec. Apr. estate Feb., 1782.

Mitchell, Joseph, dec. Settlement of estate by ex. Mary Mitchell.

Moore, Henry. Will pro. Dec., 1822. Names wife, Elizabeth and ch., John, William, Elizabeth.

Moore, James. Will pro. Aug., 1780. Names ch.. James, John, Martha Ralston, Joan McClanahan (wife Samuel McClanahan).

Montgomery, Samuel, dec. Apr. of estate, ret, March, 1777.

Mosley, Bobbett. Will pro. Nov., 1811. Names wife, Elizabeth, and ch., Henry, Mary and George. And a bro., John Mosley.

Mound, John James, dec. Dower assigned wife Harriet, Aug. 1815.

Moyer, Jacob, dec. Apr. ret. July 1795.

Mull, James. Will pro. May 1782 Names Thos. Tatum, a friend.

Murphey, Dennis. Will pro. Sept., 1808.

Names friends, James, John, Anna and Hannah. Land in Ky.

Murray, John. Will pro. Jan. 1775. Names wife, Elizabeth and ch. Richard, Martha and Charles. (Inv. calls him "Capt. John Murray".)

Muson, James, dec. Inv. ret. Nov., 1782.

Myers, Henry, dec. Inv. ret. Aug. 1821.

—N—

Nealley, John. Will pro. Aug. 1778. Names wife, Elizabeth, and ch., Robert, Andrew, John and Elizabeth Cloyd. Gr. ch. Betsy and Samuel Nealley.

Neeley, John. Will pro. Jan. 1802. Names wife, Sarah. Ex. of estate, Major Robt. Neeley.

Neeley, Robert. Will pro. Sept. 1780. Names wife, Ann, and ch., John, James, Andrew, William and Robert Neeley.

Nicholas, George. Will pro. Aug., 1812. Names wife,, Ann, and ch. names or nos. not given. Minors.

Nicholas, John - "Gent". Will pro. Oct. 1803. Names wife, Mary ,

Nofsinger, Joseph. Will pro. Sept., 1815. Names Wife Betsy, and ch., unnamed.

Norville, Thomas. Will pro. Sept. 1812. Names ch., Rebekah, Elizabeth, Nancy Young, Samuel, John, Hugh, Thomas and William.

—O—

Ocheltree, Michael. Will pro. June, 1799. Names wife, Elizabeth, and bros. and sisters. No names.

Olds, Edward. Will pro. June, 1819. Names wife, Elizabeth, and ch., Nancy Head, Elizabeth, Charles, Anderson, Luella and Henry. Gr. ch. Elizabeth Epps, dau. Patterson.

Oldshoe Jacob. dec. Apr. ret. July, 1795.

Owen, Thomas. dec. Apr. ret. Jan. 1775.

—P—

Palmer, William, dec. Apr. of estate, Nov. 1772.

Parrish, Julius, dec. Apr. of estate - wife, Betsy. Sept. 1803. ,

Pate, Jeremiah. Will pro. June, 1797. Names ch. Rhoda, Amelia, Minor, Polly Compton, Matthew, Jeremiah, Judith, John and Edward.

Patrick, Jamie. dec. Apr. ret. Dec., 1804.

Patterson, George. Will pro' April, 1789. Names wife, Margaret and ch. George and Jean, the two youngest. Others, no. or names not given.

Paul, Audley. Will pro. April, 1810. Names ch. Anna Taylor, Audley Jr., Margaret Walker, John, Rebecca Taylor, James Jane Harris, Elizabeth Defreese. Also John Walker, Crawfield Taylor and James Harris, relationship not given.

Peck, Jacob. Will pro. Oct. 1801. Names ch., Benjamin, Jacob, John, Adam, Joseph, Mary, Esther, and Hannah. (His wife was Lydia Borden.) Names son-in-law, Jacob Carper.

Peck, John. Will pro. Sept., 1802. Names wife, Mary, and ch., Susannah (wife, Allen Jones), Margaret (wife, John Sites), Ann (wife, John Campbell), Jane Peck, George, Joseph, William, Martin and Jacob C. Widow, Mary W., of son, Lewis and her son, George.

Persinger, Christopher, dec. Inv. ret. Dec, 1802.

Persinger, Jacob. Inv. ret. Dec., 1789.

Peters, Abraham, dec. Inv. ret. March, 1818.

Phillips, Samuel. Will pro. June, 1812. Names wife, Elizabeth, and ch., Samuel, Richard, Nancy, Sarah and Elizabeth. A bro., John, and Mary Anderson, relationship not stated.

Phipps, Joseph. Will pro. Feb., 11, 1772. Names ch., Joshua, Aaron, Caleb, Mary (wife Isaac Lewis of Chester Co., Pa.), Rachel (wife Owen Astin, same address), Hannah (wife Geo. Astin, Botetourt Co.), Esther Crosby (and her son Benjamin), Joseph (and his ch., Jonathan and Anne). Were Quakers.

Poage, George. Will pro. Dec., 1786. Names ch., Elizabeth Shirkey, Rachel, Margaret, Experience, Mary, George, and John, "who is six years old."

Poage, John. Will pro. Aug., 1788. Namese wife, Marthew, and ch., no. or names not given.

Poage, Robert. Will pro. Sept., 1788. Names sons, William, Robert and John. Son-in-law, Nathan Scott (wife, Sarah), and Thomas Goodson.

Poage, William, dec. Inv. of estate, 1834. Wife, Elizabeth.

Pollston, Benejamin. Will pro. Aug., 1770. Names wife, Mary, a dau., Margaret (under age) and bro., Swain Pollston.

Porter, William, dec. Apr. ret. July, 1790.

Potts, Amos. Will pro. Aug., 1780. Names wife, Hannah, and ch., John, Nathan and others, unnamed.

Preston, Jane. Will pro. July, 1813. Names ch., Polly and Thomas.

Preston, Thomas. Will pro. April, 1802. Names wife, Jane, and ch., Thomas, Anne, Mary,, Jane Snodgrass and the heirs of dec. son, John.

Price, Thomas. Will pro. 1823. Names wife, Margaret, and ch., Sophia (wife, Jacob Price), Madoriah, Agnes, Rebecca (wife, John Hank), Polly Scott, Sarah Littlepage, Margaret Bennet, and Thompson. Four others by last marriage, unnamed. Gr. ch., Alfred Holston, Sophia Price; a bro.-in-law, Thos. Beard.

Pryor, Luke. Will pro. Oct., 1783. Names wife, Susan, and bros., John, Joseph, Luke. A dec. bro's. son, John.

—R—

Reed, Rev. Joseph, dec. Inv. ret. Oct., 1813.

Reed, Samuel. Will pro. Jan., 1793. Names ch., Samuel, William, Michael, Nancy, Rachel, Elizabeth Telford, Sarah Richardson, Jane Charter, Margaret Gretton, and John.

Reed, William. Will pro. Dec., 1801,. Names wife, Ruthe, and ch., William, John, Sarah McMullin, Ruth New, Anne Knox, Margaret Persinger, Rebecca Nysonger, Thomas, Ma,ry Kinberling, and Archibald.

Reiley, Francis. Will pro. Feb., 1778. Names James Reiley and Catherine Patterson, "both of the Kingdom of Ireland, county Cavin."

Rentfro, William. Will pro. June, 1789. Names Patrick Lemon and John Targert.

Reynolds, Magdalen. Will pro. November, 1820. Names ch., James, Thomas, John, Ann Givens, Fanny Taylor, and William and his dau., Ann.

Reynolds, Thomas. Will pro. Dec., 1804. Names wife, Ann, and ch., John (eldest), Harry Byne, Sarah Loyd, Pattie King, and Betty McGee. Gr. ch., John Givin (son Jos. and Ann), Nancy Ann Taylor. (Note: Wife is evidently the Magdelena above.)

Reynolds, William, dec. Apr. ret. Feb., 1796.

Richards, Richard, dec. Apr. ret. April, 1803.

Richardson, Samuel. Will pro. Oct., 1821. Names son, John. Other ch., but names not given.

Richey, John. Will pro. Aug., 1780. Names wife, Sarah, and ch., James, Stephen, John, Mary and Aunice.

Rinehart, Francis. Will pro. Jan. 1814. Names wife, Rebakeh, and ch., John, and others, unnamed.

Ripp, Frederick, dec. Apr. ret. Feb., 1790.

Robinet, Samuel, dec. Inv. ret. April, 1772.

Robinson, David. Will pro. June, 1787. Names wife, Catron, and ch., William, George, James, Pricilla, Jane, Cat,herine, Mary, Elizabeth, Ann, Annabal, Phebe, and Prudence. Son-in-law, William Mc. Donald.

Robinson, Elizabeth, dec. Inv. ret. Aug., 1772.

Rowland, James. Will pro. June, 1805. Names wife, Margaret, and ch., Mary, Elizabeth, Jane, Margaret, Agnes, Prudence, George, James, William and Robert.

Rowland, James. Will pro. April, 1819. Names wife, Sarah, and ch., Charlotte and James.

Rowland, Robert. Will pro. Feb. 1782. Names ch., James, Thomas, George. Heirs of dec. son, William. Only one name given, Robert.

Rowland, Thomas. Will pro. Aug., 1814. Names wife, Mary, and ch., Jesse, Silas, Joel, George (land in Jessimine Co., Ky.), Milly Gilmore, William and David (land in Ky.).

Rowland, William. Will pro. March, 1777. Non-cup. will. Equal div. between all his children. No names.

Ruddell, Cornelius. Will pro. April, 1798. Names wife, Ingebo, and ch, Andrew, John, Stephen, Chear Reader, Deborah Rutledge, Catherine Sangler, and Elizabeth Alcorn. Niece, Ingobo, dau. bro., George.

Rute, George. Will pro. Sept. 1823. Names ch., Catherine "alias Shute", Rosanna "alias French," George, Christinah "alias Dasher," Jacob, John, Michael. Gr. dau., Sally French.

—S—

Savour, Elizabeth. Will pro. June, 1790. Names Julies Webb, Sr.

Scott, James. Will pro. Sept. 1783. Names wife, Esther, and ch., William, Samuel, and four daughters.

Scott, Nathan. Will pro. Oct. 1819. Names ch., Robert, William, Jane (wife David Short), Sarah (wife Phil Whitmore), Isabella, Peggy (wife Andrew Mellon). He states that these 4 daus. "have removed to western country." Also Mary, Rebecca, Nathan, John, James and Joseph.

Seacat, Elizabeth. Will pro. June, 1824. Leaves estate for upkeep of graves of herself and dec. husband, George Seacat.

Seacrist, John. Will pro. June, 1815. Names wife, ..., and ch., Daniel and others, unnamed.

Sevear, Casper. Will pro. Feb., 1782. Names wife, and ch., Henry, Casper and John.

Samblin (Shanklin?), Aaron. Will pro. Feb.,

1789. Names ch., William, Aaron, George, Jesse and Mary. Gr. Ch., George and Cittle, ch. of Mary.

Shanklin, Robert. Will pro. Oct., 1800. Names wife, Agnes, and ch., John, William, Robert, Andrew, Catherin, Richard and Elizabeth (and her son, Absolum).

Shanklin, Robert, dec. Apr. of estate Feb., 1802.

Shanks, David. Will pro. Aug., 1821. Names wife, Temain, and ch., William, David, Thomas, James, Lewis, Carey, Cassey, George Washington. A sister, Sarah.

Sharkey, Patrick. Will pro. March, 1786. Names wife, Anne, and sons, James, John and Patrick.

Sharp, Edward. Will pro. 1770. Names wife, ..., and ch., John, Anthony, another, no name. Father-in-law, John McClellon and wife's bro., John. In 1786 an account gives wife's name as Jane and ch. as Anthony, John, and Annis.

Shaver, Andrew. Will pro. March, 1816. Names wife, Wisula, and ch., Andrew, Betsy, Sally, Lucy and others, unnamed. A bro., Adam.

Shaver, Peter. Will pro. April, 1798. Names father, Andrew, and a bro., Andrew.

Shewsberry, Dabney, dec. Apr. ret. Feb., 1803.

Short, Jacob. Inv. ret. June, 1805.

Shrido, John, dec. Inv. ret. Sept., 1772.

Sigle, Nancy, dec. Sales bill Oct., 1811.

Simmons, Jacob, dec. Inv. ret. Feb., 1789.

Simms, Ignatius, Jr., of Charlotte Co., Md. Will pro. Nov., 1786. Names mother, Sarah, and a bro., James, and sisters, Matingly, Sarah and Ann Fowler. Niece and nephew, John and Maddox Simms.

Skidmore, James. Will pro. Dec., 1807. Names wife, ..., and ch., Ann, Joseph, John, Randolph, James and Sarah.

Skillern, Elizabeth. Will pro. Oct., 1808. Names dau. Nancy.

Skillern, George. Will pro. April, 1804. Names wife, Elizabeth, and ch., William Preston, Elizabeth Beale, Peggy Beale and Nancy.

Skillern, William. Will pro. Feb., 1817. Names wife, ..., and son, George. (Note: Settlement shows other children as John, Rebecca, wife of Wm. Anderson of Bledsoe County, Tenn., William, 3rd and James.

Sloan, Archibald. Will pro. Oct., 1804. Names wife, Nelly, and ch., Mattie, Elizabeth, George, Sarah Kirk, Rosannah McClendish, Nelly Skidmore, Polly Ferguson, David and James.

Smiley, Walter. Will pro. June, 1807. Names

ch., Alexander, George, Daniel, James and Nancy. Says Nancy has six children.

Smith, David, dec. Apr. of estate ret. July, 1782.

Smith, James, dec. Apr. of estate ret. March, 1780.

Smith, John. Will pro. March, 1783. Names wife, Margaret, and ch., James, Abraham, Henry, and John. Mentions his officers claim warrant.

Smith, John. Will pro. April, 1806. Names wife, Mary, and son, Samuel.

Smith, William, dec. Apr. ret. Nov., 1786.

Smyth, Rev. Ad. Will pro. July, 1786. Names ch., Nancy V. Moxley, Alexander and others - no no. or names. Also father and step-mother - no names.

Smythe, James. Will pro. June, 1790. "Of the Kingdom of Ireland." Names bro., Alexander. Was son of Benjamin Allen Smythe, dec.

Smythe, Jane, dec. Apr. of estate ret. Feb., 1820.

Snider, Jacob. Will pro. Sept., 1821. Names ch., by 1st wife, Elizabeth Kelly, Mary, Molly Felty, John, George, Christian, Barberry and Eve. Names Jacob, Flany, Nickolas and Lilly, relationship not given, but possible ch. of last marriage.

Snider, Philip. Will pro. Sept., 1803. Names brother, Henry, and sister, unnamed.

Snodgrass, Elizabeth, dec. Inv. ret. Feb., 1783.

Snodgrass, Joseph. Will pro. Oct., 1782. Names wife, Hannah, and ch., Robert, Joseph, Lydia Cammeron, Margaret McClanahan, Hannah, Rebecca (wife John Potts), Phebe Baker and Isaac. A gr.son, Joseph Potts.

Snodgrass, Joseph. Will pro. Sept., 1809. Names wife, Mary, and ch., Robert, John, Joseph, Caroline, William, Elizabeth St. Clair, George, Bartley, Henry and Polly. "Ex bro-in-law," John Walker.

Snodgrass, Robert. Will pro. Nov., 1806. Names ch., Tilgman, William Adams, Sabra, Elizabeth, Jenny and Miranda. Brothers, Joseph and Tilgman West.

Snodgrass, William. Will pro. June, 1791. Names wife, Isabella, and ch., Joseph, James, William, John, Susan Tweedy, Jain Fisher, Margaret Steel, Isabella McClenahan, and Elinor George.

Spechard, Philip, dec. Inv. ret. Jan., 1793.

Spillar, Jacob. Will pro. March, 1820. Names wife, Fanny, and ch., Michael, Barbara Cram, Daniel, Elizabeth Peters, Hannah My........, and Magdalene.

Star, Henry, dec. Apr. ret. June, 1810.

Statler, Abraham. Will pro. May, 1813. Names ch., Abraham, John and Elizazbeth Right. Son-in-law, John Write, and John Good.

Stuart, James, dec. Inv. ret. Dec., 1803.

Stuart, Robert, dec. Inv. ret. Dec., 1819.

Switzer, Henry. Will pro. June, 1798. Names wife, Chloe, and ch., William (eldest son), Nathan, Thomas, John, Mary and Joseph.

Swittzer Nathan, dec. Inv. ret. Oct., 1842. Settlement of est. names ch., Thomas, George, Jonathan, Bartlett, Pricilla, Rachel, Lewis and Madison Monroe.

Switzer, William. Will pro. Feb., 1812. Names wife, Nancy, and ch., William, Sarah, Cloe, James. Bros., John and Joseph.

Sympson Solomon. Will pro. Feb., 1785. Names wife, Margaret, and ch., Solomon and Elizabeth.

—T—

Tate, Nathaniel, dec. Apr. estate ret. March, 1810.

Taylor, John. Will pro. June, 1812. Names wife, Mary, and ch., Andrew, Elizabeth (wife, Tom Price), John, Isaac, Thomas and James. Heirs of dec. dau. Mary. Their father, Moses Bonont, dec., also.

Teel, Thomas. Will pro. Jan., 1824. Names wife, Martha, and ch., Henry, Betsy Johnson, Peter, John and Jacob.

Thomas Loderwick. Will pro. Sept., 1778. Names ch., Magdalene Rennils, Margaret Christian, Elizabeth, Abraham, Mary and Catherine.

Thomas, Richard. Will pro. Oct., 1782. Names mother, Mildred Thomas, sister, Sarah and bros. James and George.

Thompson, John. Will pro. June, 1822. Names wife, Judith, and ch., Bartlett, John W., Creed T., Anderson, Elizabeth Eubank (wife Elias M.) and Mary Shirkey.

Tosh, Jonathan. Will pro. Feb., 1782. Names wife, Dina, ch., Nancy, and one unborn. Bro., James, and cousin, Jonathan Tosh.

Tosh, Jonathan, dec. Settlement estate May, 1812. Names wife, Elizabeth, and ch. Jonathan, Jean (wife, Wm. Lewis) and Thomas.

Tosh, Thomas. Will pro. Feb. 1778. Names wife, Mary, and ch., Mary, Jonathan, and son-in-law, James Crawford.

Tosh, William. Will pro. Feb., 1773. Names bros., Jonathan, James, and sister, Jean.

Trimble, James. Will pro. April, 1776. Names wife, Sarah, and ch., John, Isaac, Moses, James, Alexander, William, Agnes, Sarah, Rachel, Jean McClure. A bro., Moses Trim-

ble.

Trisslar, Henry, dec. Jan., 1820. Div. of land names heirs: William, Jacob, Henry, Peter, Sally, George, Moses, Nancy, Michael, Barbara (wife, Wm. Persigner), Mary (wife, Adam Quickle), Catherine (wife, George Mallow), and Elizazbeth (wife, Jacob Pence).

Trout, John. Will pro. Dec., 1816. Names wife, Elizabeth, andch., John, Philip, Elizabeth, Michel, Emanuel, Jacob and Rosannah.

Turman, Benjamin. Will pro. Oct., 1784. Names wife, Frances, and ch., Charles, George, John, Elizabeth, James, Ignasus, Benjamin, William, Mary, Ann and Frances.

Turner, James. Will pro. April, 1823. Names wife, Sally, and ch., no. or names not given.

—V—

Vanbibber, Isaac, dec. Inv. ret. April, 1776.

Vineyard, Christian. Will pro. June, 1798. Names wife, Christinah, and ch., Christian, John, and other, unnamed. Will written in German. Translated before recording.

Vineyard, Christian, dec. Division of land, May, 1819. (Same as above?) Names heirs: Nicholas Taylor, John, Peter, Nancy, William, Christian, Abraham, Elizabeth (wife James Bryant), Catherine (wife Wm. Stuart) and Tabler.

Vineyard, Christinah, dec. Inv. ret. Feb., 1805.

—W—

Waddle, James. Will pro. June, 1809. Names Anny McCleur.

Wadle, Martin. Will pro. March, 1783. Names wife, Kathrean, and ch., Benjamin and Barbara, wife of John Phisichimer.

Waggoner, James, dec. Adm. of estate, his wife, Mary, Sept., 1819.

Walker, Alexander. Will pro. Aug., 1771. (Non-cup. will) Names sister, Martha Mineely, bro., John Walker, and two nieces and nephew "in Carolina." He "died Saturday about ten o'clock in the morning July 6, A. D. 1771."

Walker, Henry. Will pro. 1803. Names wife, ..., and ch., Andrew, William, Robert, Henry, Archabald, Mary, Joseph and George.

Walker, James, dec. Inv. ret. Oct., 1823.

Walker, William. Will pro. Sept., 1810. Names ch., John, Esther, George, James, William - "and my daughter-in-law, Martha Walker, equally." Son-in-law, Thomas Harmon, gr.-

sons, William (son of John) and William (son of William).

Watkins, John. Will pro. Oct., 1784. Names wife, Elinor, and ch., Joel, Jonathan, Agnes, Mary.

Wax Henry. Will pro. 1797. Names wife, Catherine, and children, grandchildren, and sons-in-law," Peter, John, Henry, Jacob, Mary, Christine, Mandilson, Hannah, Hetty and Susannah Wax, Mary Boyer, George Etter, Henry Price, and Margaret Hatsimpillar. Does not distinguish between them.

Wax, Peter, dec. Inv. ret. July, 1804.

Weaver, Leonard. Will pro. July, 1800. Names Conrad (eldest), Catherine, Barbara and Leonard, his children.

Welch, Thomas. Will pro. Oct., 1802. Names wife, Jean, and sons of his son, Thomas.

Wernor, Daniel. Will pro. June, 1802. Names ch., George (and his son, Daniel), Mary Lake (her ch. Frances and Daniel), Anne Boyer, William, Sarah, Philip, and Aaron.

White, Peter, dec. Apr. ret. Oct., 1810. June 1812, dower aseslegned Mary Campbell from est. "of her first husband, Peter White."

Whitley, Paul. Wiell pro. May, 1772. Names wife, Jane, and ch., Michael, Sarah, Moses, Thomas, Anne, Samuel and Paul - all minors. Names a sister, Ann.

Willis, John, dec. Inv. ret. July, 1773.

Wilson, Eliezabeth. Will pro. Nov., 1824. Names dau., Sarah.

Wilson, John. Will pro. May, 1823. Names wife, Elizabeth, and ch., Ann, Thomas, Pricilla, Sarah, James and John.

Wilson, Matthew. Will pro. Dec., 1795. Names wife, Mary, and ch., Thomas, John (of Ky.), Steel, Samuel, Matthew (of Ky.), Jennt, Betsy, Polly, Sally and Nancy.

Wilson, Patrick. Will pro. April, 1774. Names ch., William, Alexander, Moses, Andrew, John, and Thomas.

Wilson, Richard. Will pro. May, 1779. Names

wife, Mary, and ch., William and Thomas.

Wilson, William. Will pro. May, 1823. Names wife, Rebecca, and ch., John L., David J. and others, no. or names not given.

Witturs, John. Will pro. Oct., 1805. Names wife, Elizabeth, and children. No names.

Woods, Andrew. Will pro. Aug., 1781. Names ch., James, Andrew, Archabald, Robert, Martha, Mary, Elizabeth Cloyd, and Rebekah Kelly. (Wife was Martha.)

Woods, Arthur, dec. Apr. ret. Sept., 1773.

Woods, Jane. Will pro. June, 1816 (non-cup. will). Died Apr. 3, 1816. Names ch., Margaret and William. Gr.dau., Demarius Flint.

Woods, Jonathan. Will pro. Feb., 1804. Names bro., James, of Montgomery Co., and John Woods, son of his bro., Jeremiah.

Woods, Joseph. Will pro. Apr., 1816. Names ch., Carlos, Edward, Thomas, Joseph, James, Anna, Mary Stull, Martha and Sally.

Woods, Michael. Will pro. March, 1777. Names wife, Anne, and ch., Jane Buster, Susannah Cowan, Samuel, Elizabeth Shepherd, William, Magdalene Campbell, David, Martha and Sarah.

Wright, Peter. Will pro. Dec., 1793. Names wife, Jane, and ch., Peter, Elizabeth Sprowl, Mary Smyth, Rebecca Kirkhead, Thomas (and his ch., Jane and James), Agnes Clark, Jane Estill, and Rachel Proctor.

Wrightman, John. Will pro. Sept., 1810. Names ch., John, Samuel, Michael, Daniel, Solomon, Mary, Christinia Lohre.

—Y—

Young, Isaac (of Augusta Co., Va.). Will pro. June, 1818. Names bros., John, Thomas, Hugh F. Had sisters, Mary, Sarah, Catherine. He was son fo Hugh, and grandson of Isaac Young (O.B.B.).

—Z—

Zeglar, David. Will pro. Jan., 1812. Names ch., Elizabeth, and others, unnamed.

Some Revolutionary Records of
Botetourt Co., Va. - Aug., 1782

The following is an exact copy of original records found in the basement of the court-house, in Fincastle, Botetourt County, Virginia. Some names were too faded to be legible, and a part was missing.

"At a meeting of the field officers this thirty-first of August, 1782, for the county of Botetourt, for the purpose of carrying into Exercution this state's quota of Troops to serve the United States Army for the Term of three years, or during the War. Present, George Skillern, County Lieut., Colo., Wm. McClenechan, Lieut. Colo., Patr. Lockhart, Majr., James Breckenridge appointed Clerk, who took the Oath by Law required. Adam Peck appointed Martial."

"List of Capt. Eson's Company amounting to 45 men returned:

Capt. Martin's Do..Do..30 men..Do
Capt. Cartmill's Do..Do 44 men..Do
Capt. Pryor's Do..Do..42 men..Do
Capt. Looney's Do..Do..40 men..Do
Capt. May's Do..Do..77 men..Do
Capt. Watterson's Do..Do..36 men..Do
Capt. Galloway's Do..Do..43 men..Do
Capt. Neely's Do..Do..52 men..Do
Capt. Barnett's Do..Do..45 men..Do
Capt. Mill's Do..Do..43 men..Do
Capt. Pauling's Do..Do..35 men..Do
Capt. Robinson's Do..Do..68 men..Do
Capt. Smith's Do..Do..33 men..Do
Capt. Taylor's Do..Do..43 men..Do
Capt. Ballar's Do..Do..33 men..Do."

"Ordered that the following Persons in Capt. Eson's Company - viz: Capt. Samuel Eson, Christopher Richards, Richard Beckett, Thomas Gee, John Gee, Joshua Morris, John Patterson, John Hungate, William Hungate, Bristole Mathews, John Plumbley, John Nale, Mathew Scott, William Terry, Joseph Huff, of Capt. Eson's Company be considered the First District.

That Lt. Thomas Goodson, Jonathan Tully, Jonathan Graham, John Loyd, John Harth, Josiah Terry, Vitchel Clarke, Thomas Ashby, Amos Graham, William Spurlock, Benjamin Turmon, Ignatious Turman, Macajah Keeth, James McCutchen, of Capt. Eson's Company, be considered the Second District.

That Lt. William Goodson, George Ingle, Danl. Howell, William Dalton, Hezekiah Summer, Peter Reid, Charles Simmonds, Obediah Dickinson, Richard Newton, Charles Thurman, David Thomas, Martin Branham, of Capt. Eson's Company, be considered as the Third District.

Ordered, that the following persons in Capt. Martin's Company - viz: Capt. Joshua Martin, David Iddings, Jonathan Harrison, Christopher Cooper, Robert Beavers, Joshua Wilson, John Cooper, William Seagraves, David Alley, Job Hale, William Likens, John Hays, Thomas Lutterall, John Huff, Jesse Chamberlan, of Capt. Martin's Company considered as the Fourth District.

That Lt. William Terry, Robert McElhaney, Joseph Cole, James Cooper, John McClelan, William Hays, Paul Deweese, Thomas Quigley, William Allen, William Deormand, John Henderson, John Jones, John Long, John King, Zadock Martin, of Capt. Martin's Company, be considered as the Fifth District.

That Ensign James Raeburn, Valentine Thrash, John Davies, Thomas Davies, William Davies, James Davies, Solomon Stephens, Thomas Gash, Joseph Ackerley, Thomas Ackerley, Abrm. Ackerley, John Raeburn, of Capt. Barnett's and John Ball, James Dodly, and Peter Freeman, of Capt. Eson's Company be considered as the Sixth District.

That Colo Hugh Crocket of Capt James Barnett's Company, Capt. James Barnett, William Barnett, John Kent, Thomas Barnett, John Barnett, William McNéeley, Peter Brooks, George Madison, Jervis Brooks, William Ewing, William Stapleton, Henry Coleman, Solomon George, be considered as the Seventh District.

That Lt. William Bryan, Moses Dunlap, Malcolm Hunter, Danl. Britt, John Britt, James Britt, Wm. McKinny, Thomas Jones, William Taylor, Joseph Taylor, John Stephens, Nathan Davies, William Owens, Thos. Gulliam, James Coffee, of Capt. Barnett's Company, be considered as the Eighth District.

That William Walton, John Lewis, Lt. Andrew Lewis, John Lowe, John Walton, James Bryan (millwght), Thomas Kersey, James Bryan, Jun., William Bryan, Jun., John Billups, William Bryan, Jesse Hudson, of Capt. Lewis' Company and George Severt, James Smith, Robert Brown and Michael Yoakam, of Capt. Barnett's Company, be considered as the Ninth District.

That Thomas Lewis, Joseph Carlton, Hugh Alexander, David Wilson, James Simpson, Samuel Crawford, Bryan Mooney, William Greenlee, Alexr. Greenlee, John Ingram, William Ingram, Alexr. Ingram, John Henry, Thomas McElheney, of Capt. Lewis' Company be considered as the Tenth District.

That Andrew Armstrong, Thomas Armstrong, John Johnson, George Hanna, William John Johnston, Thomas Hannon, of Capt. Neeley's Company, and William Poage, John Picklesimon, Jacob Picklesimon, John Peydon, James Paydon, Robert Smithy, Joseph Sprightley, Absolom Smyth, William Henry, be considered as the Eleventh District.

That Capt. James Neeley, Lt. Robert Neeley, Wm. Neeley, James Tosh, Samuel (Lemuel) Andrews, John Griffith, John Neeley, Saml. Boswell, Thomas Brown, John Reynolds, Jas. Trimble, John Kelley, John Hartman, George Kelley, Peter Corbin, of Capt. Neeley's Company, be considered as the Twelfth District.

That Toliver Craig, William Johnson, Saml. McElhaney, Pierce Daniel, Eson Hannon, Nathan Scott, William Crawford, Thomas Crawford, Hugh Crawford, Jonathan Tosh, John Terry, Miles Terry, William Horton . . . . .n Craig, Joel Richardson, of Capt. Neeley's Company be considered as the Thirteenth District.

That Thomas Brown, John Horton, Colo. William McClenehan, Lowe Snowden, John Henry, Andrew Tilford, Jared Gladden, John Bandy, William Roberts, John Hammond, Robert Clark, John Kinsey, Saml. Witherington, Thomas Protherson, Peter Cogar, of Capt. Neeley's Company be considered as the Fourteenth District.

That Capt. John Johnson, Isaac Robinson, Richard Bandy, Francis Golston, Saml. Crawford, Dnl. McNeel, John Hankins, Moses Tulles, of Capt. Pawling's Company, and Edward Wright, John Snowden, Jacob Snowden, William Pruitt, William Walker, Joseph Mason, James Mason, of Capt. Neeley's Company be considered as the Fifteenth District.

Ordered that the following persons in Capt. Pawling's Company-viz: Henry Pawling, Joseph Richardson, Danile Howell, Thomas Dalzeil, Ezekiel Howard, Thomas West, Benn West, Resin West, Abner Howell, Saml. Depew, David Jones, James Stewart, Jun.,

Peter Cline, of Capt. Pawling's Company be considered the Sixteenth District.

That Lt. Francis Graham, William Campbell, William Worrell, Thomas Madison, Edw. Summers, John Briggs, John Howell, John Vinyard, Thomas Thompson, John Tumly, Robert Baker, George Graham, Danl. Hickson, John Runnion, Robert Cummins, of Capt. Pawling's Company be considered as the Seventeenth District.

And that the following persons in Capt. Henry Watterson's Company - viz: Joseph Raeburn, William Robinson, Frans Daugherty, Thomas Wilson, Robert Shields, Thomas Shields, John McNeely, David McNeely, Richard Stephens, Isaac Richards, William Pitzer, William Bones, Rene LeForce, George McNeely, William Thomas, be considered as the Eighteenth District.

That James Wilson, William Daugherty, John Green, John Raeburn, James Woods, Robert Henderson, Robert King, John Henderson, John Van Leer, James McGee, David McGee, George Rutledge and John Rutledge, of Capt. Watterson's Company be considered as the Nineteenth District.

And the following persons in Capt. Galloway's Company, viz: Capt. John Galloway, George Greene, John Wiley, Field Jarvis, Mitchel Porter, Thomas Tipton, William Tipton, Jonathan Taylor, Henry Cartay, John Jarvis, Jacob Persinger, John Persinger, Crane Brush, James Wright, Christian Persinger, John Persinger, of Capt. Galloway's Company be considered as the Twentieth District.

That John Lewis, John Herbert, William Hammon, Drury Hammon, James McMullin, Drury Smith, John McCallister, James McCallister, David Rees, John Rees, Wm. Loague David Tate, Jun., James Brown, and John Neil of Capt. Galloway's Company, be considered the Twenty-First District.

That Lt. Wallace Estill, Owen Neil, Thomas Carpenter, David Glasburn, Jesse Bennett, John Robinson, Richard Manlays, Joseph Hunter, Elisha Knox, William Hunter, Abrm Dicks, David Dicks, Richard McEllister, Garret McCallister, of Capt. Galloway's Company to be considered as the Twenty-second District.

Ordered that the persons in the following company's; viz - Capt. John Baird, Joseph Server, Gasper Faught, Powell Faught, James Stewart, John Clendennon, William Mays, William Verner, Saml Baird, Joseph Thompson, Barnaby Rupe, Chisholm Griffin, Robert Beaty, to be considered as the Twenty-fourth District.

That Capt. John Ballar, Thomas Mulholland, and William Craig, Ezekiel Trotter, James Scott, Adam Kimberland, John Votair, John Scott, Robert Armstrong, John McDuff, Thomas Wall, Dnl. FitzPatrick, James Morris, John Morris, Roger Morning, of Capt. Ballar's Company, be considered as the Twenty-fifth District.

That Lt. James Armstrong, Moses Mann, John Jones, John Kincade, Robert Kincade, William Kincade, James Davis, Thos. Barbery, Edward McCallister, Wm. Corder, Wm. Smith, David Robinson, James Robinson, of Capt. Ballar's Company be considered as the Twenty-sixth District.

That William Wright, Thomas McCallister, Wm Sprowl, Robert Viers, Moses Mann, Jun., Esau Mann, Joseph Clark, Jeremiah Carpenter, Timothy Smith, David Smith, Bryan Smith, George Clark, David McMurry, Thomas McMurry, Wm. McMurry, of Capt. Baird's Company, be considered as the Twenty-seventh District.

That George Frazer, Wm Frazer, Joseph Frazer, James Gillilan, Jacob C......ms, Felty Miller, Robert Hall, Joseph Haynes, Benn Haynes, William Haynes, George Cairns, of Capt Beard's Company, and Christopher Jackson, George Stull, Spencer Humphreys, Spencer Hany of Capt Pryor's Company, to be considered as the Twenty-eighth District.

That Capt. Joseph Pryor, Abel Roberts. John Pitzers, Joseph Dameron, Charles Stewart, Alexr Simpson, John Johnson, Charles King, Zacheriah King, John Ocheltree, Luke Pryor, John Gill, Edward Gill, Vincent Sorrells, of Capt. Pryor's Company to be considered the Twenty-ninth District.

That Ensign Uriah Humphreys, Jonathan Taylor, Jeremiah Bell, Francis Rawson, Seabritt Sillars, Andrew Crawford, Jun., James Crawford, Josiah Crawford, Jun., Joel Hanell, Henry Gibson, Thomas Hart, Jeremiah Scott, Peter McCallister, James Sharkey, Niels Sharkey, of Capt. Pryor's Company be considered the Thirtieth District.

That Lt. Hugh Allen, John Allen, Leonard Shoemaker, David Henderson, John Bennett, Peter Circle, Philip Myers, John Howard, Joseph Miller, John Crawford, Jun., of Capt. Pryor's Company, and Walter Lindsay, Malcolm McClure, of Capt. Smith's Company be considered the Thirty-first District.

That George Hutchenson, Capt. James Smith, John Sascalled (?), David Worldley, Wm. Hutcheson, Thomas Hutcheson, Saml. McClure, John Wilson, William Wilson, Wm.

Cleney, Thomas Reid, Thomas Anderson Joseph Titus, Colo George Skillers, of Capt. Smith's Company be considered the Thirty-second District.

That Joseph Kyle, Elijah Vansandt, Joseph McFerran, Samuel McFerran, Samuel McFerran Jun., Martin McFerran, William Kyle, John Grimley, Elisha Vansandt, Arthur Williams, Palsar Kimberling, John Blagg, Ephriam, Russell, Wm. Ritchie, Edward Stevens, of Capt. Smith's Company be considered the Thirty-third District.

That the following persons in Capt. Cartmill's Company, viz: David Wallace, John Henry, Michael Ocheltree, Christopher Hurst, Samuel Woods, John Wingfield, Wm .Baston, Henry Baston, William Sutton, Henry Cartmill, Thomas Suvill, Patrick Dunn, Jas. McCarrell, Thomas Harrison, be considered as the Thirty-fourth District.

That William Campbell, Joseph Skidmore, James Wallace, Sam'l Mitchell, Joseph McBride, Nath'l Jones, Saml Carter, Chas. Hoggs, John Wilson, Rosmus Jones, Wm. Taylor, Canfield Taylor, John Fafilee, David Rush, John Woodward, of Capt. Cartmill's Company be considered as the Thirty-fifth District.

That John Black, James Black, Alexr Black, James Ferguson, William Cherry, Jacob Vandine, John Luke, Isaac Depew, Wm. Neil, Wm. Dempsey, Thomas Dickerson, of Capt Cartmill's Company, and Benn Kelly, Jas. McComb, Jesse McComb, Thomas Armstrong, of Capt Smith's Company, be considered as the Thirty-sixth District.

That Capt. John Mills, William Anderson, James Mills, Wm. Allen, Thos. Crow, Henry White, George Wattwood, John Painter, Wm. Franklin, Joshua Phipps, Joseph Jenkins, Wm. Aston, Wm. Martin, Joseph Martin, Thomas Ruddsill, of Capt. Mill's Company, be considered as the Thirty-seventh District.

That James Lauderdale, William Louderdale, John Louderdale, John Wood, Horn (?) Compton, Andrew Clark, John Layman, Isaac Kelly, Lawrence Young, Thomas Fitswater, Charles Stewart, Wm. Switzer, Mathew Wilson, Colo Thomas Rowland, James Vicars, of Capt. Mills' Company be considered the Thirty-eighth District.

That William McClelan, Samuel Walker, Joseph Walker, James Ewing, James Moore, John Moore, Samuel McClenechan, Mathew Ralston, John Pryor, Joseph Pryor, Archibald Woods, Andrew Woods, Samuel Todd, Thomas Miller, of Capt. Mills' Company, be considered the Thirty-ninth District.

That James Breckenridge, Capt. James Robinson, Andrew Neely, Reuben Green, John McElwain, Joseph Darr, Michl Cloyd, Edward Springer, William Dunn, Thomas Preston, Saml. Coburn, Francis Smith, William Ryan, Harris Ryan Stephen May, of Capt. Robinson's Company to be considered the Fortieth District.

That John Neely, William Breckenridge, John Breckenridge, jun., John McRoberts, Samuel McRobebrts, Alexander McRobebrts, Curtis Anderson, Thomas Miller, Allen Gulliford, John Barton, Stephen Hughs, Robert Hammett, John Curdy, Joseph Emmons, Isaac Emmons, to be considered the Forty-first district. . . . . . .

That Jacob Carper, Davis Attactchuson, ... Bryan, Samuel Young, John Hewett, William McClenechan, David Hall, Joseph Carroll, Wm. George, Alexander Hanna, Joseph Hanna, Robert Caldwell, Patrick Sherkey, to be considreed the Forty-second District.

(Forty-third District missing)

Isaac VanMetre, Robert Harvey, Wm. Hawkins, John Gillespie, John Peck, Robert Rowland, James Strian, David Wilson, James McClelechan, Samuel Baldwin, John Sherkey, Nathan Switzer, Nathan . . . ., Jesse Robinett, Charles Scott, Alex. Guthhrey, be considered the Forty-forth District.

That Thomas Gillis, William Cox, David Smith, George Patterson, Robert McMullen, William Robinson, of Capt. Watterson's Company, and Uriah Rector, William Crawford, John Medlock, Barton Mcferson, Charles Medlock, Berry Bedlock, Mack Rector, Tobias Tilghman, Thomas Goodson, of Capt. Looney's Company, be considered the Forty-fifth District.

(First part gone) . . William McClenehan, Sturdy Jones, Samuel Adams, Thomas Hackett, Thomas Middleton, Jr. Walter Gray, John Keith, John Hale, Alexr Martin, Absolom Looney, Jacob Middleton, Michl O'Hair. En. Jno. Hawkins, of Capt. Looney's Company, be considered as the Forty-sixth Distr.

That Lt. John Reynolds, James Runnolds, Moses Preston, Jonathan Martin, Saml C - in, Hawkins Thisby, Augustine Webb, Richard Ramsey, Benj Ramsey, Thomas Williams, John Withers, William Medlock, John Middleton, Samuel Wilson, John Wade, of Capt. Looney's Company to be considered the Forty seventh District.

The 48th, 49th, and 50th District lists missing.

That Lt William McDonald, Joseph Snodgrass, Jr., David McClenachan, Robert Armstrong, Charles Allison, Isaac Snodgrass, John Cummins, Robert Kerr, Charles McFadden, Edward McDonald, Robert Snodgrass, (son to Joseph), James King, William McNeely, John Ross, Jr., of Capt. David May's Company to be considered the Fifty-first District.

That Lt. Joseph Snodgrass, Henry (?) Parrott, Alexd McDonald, Robert Henderson Randolph McDonald, Thomas Gibbins (Cribbins?) James Snodgrass, Jun., William Snodgrass, Jun., John Wrightsman, John Miller, Elijah Smith, John Cox, Fight Wysong, Jacob Smith of Capt. May's Company be considered the Fifty-second District.

That Lt. Alexr. Smiley, Robert Wilson, William Craddock, Andrew Wilson, Thomas Wilson, Jun., John Wilson, George Smiley, David Little, James Corbet, Fredk Brightold, Mathew Cooney, James Snodgrass (called little), Robert Snodgrass (son of James), William Little, James McGuire, of Capt. May's Company to be considered the Fifty-third District.

That John Drakie (Drahie?), John Neeley, Daniel Goodwin, Joseph Ward, Thomas Howell, William Brickey, Jno. McClelan, Robt. Scanlin, Elias Oliver (Oiven?), Samuel Phillips, John Brickey, Peter Brickey, Samuel Garwood, Samuel LeForce, Jno B....ns, of Capt. May's Company be considered the Fifty-fourth Dist.

That James Wills, William Wills, Jun., Andrew Wills, James Evans, Robert Wilson Senr., Samuel Kerr, Jno Miller (Cove), Allen Cox, James Peerie, Gasper Lewer, James Ward, Peter Conrod, William Hill, William Peerie, William Wallace, Daniel Jones, Robert McMullen, of Capt. May's Company, be considered the Fifty-fifth District.

That James Tate, Jesse T...., William R.. ..d, Rowland Ross, of Capt. May's Company, and James Hulie (?), William Macmuth, William Hanson, John Hanson, Robt. McNeeley, Jonathan Wood, Robt. Louderdale, James McCreery, James Neely, of Capt. Mill's Company, and William Dodd and Robt Harris, of Capt. Harris's Company be considered the Fifty-sixth District. The Last District.

Note: Some of the names were not legible. Some were badly faded. In every instance those letters appearing, were copied. When in doubt, the most likely translation is used with the next best in parenthesis.